Zombielzebub
Hell's Invasion

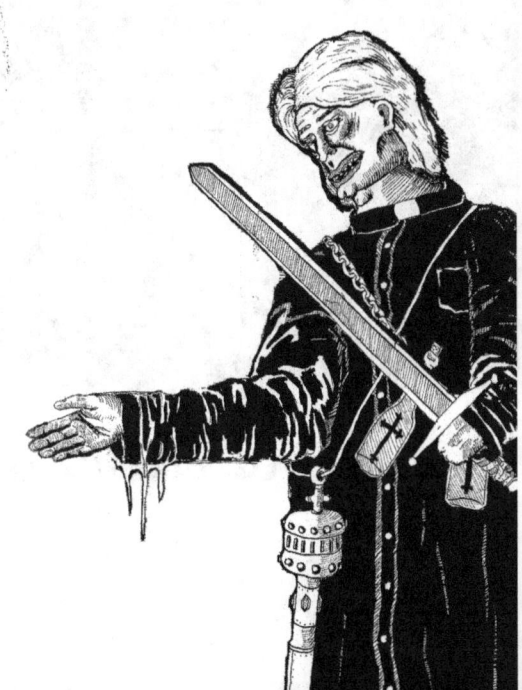

CREATED BY: JOHN BECKMANN

stampedepress.com

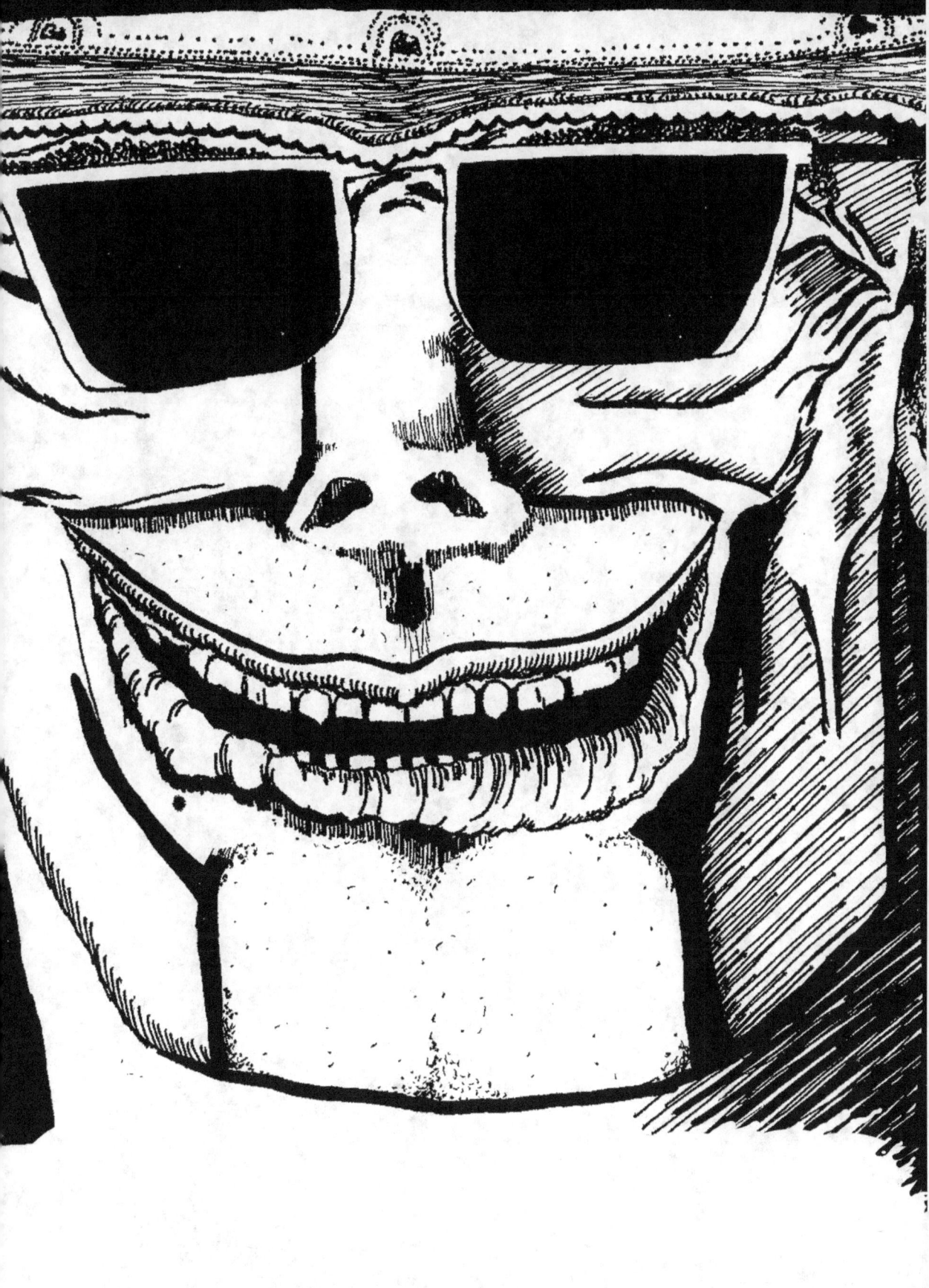

Publisher and Design
JOHN F. BECKMANN

stampedePress.com

Published by
Stampede Press
214 NE 11th Ave
Faribault, Minnesota 55021

www.stampedepress.com

ISBN-13: 978-0615741024

Designed by John F. Beckmann

1st edition December 2012

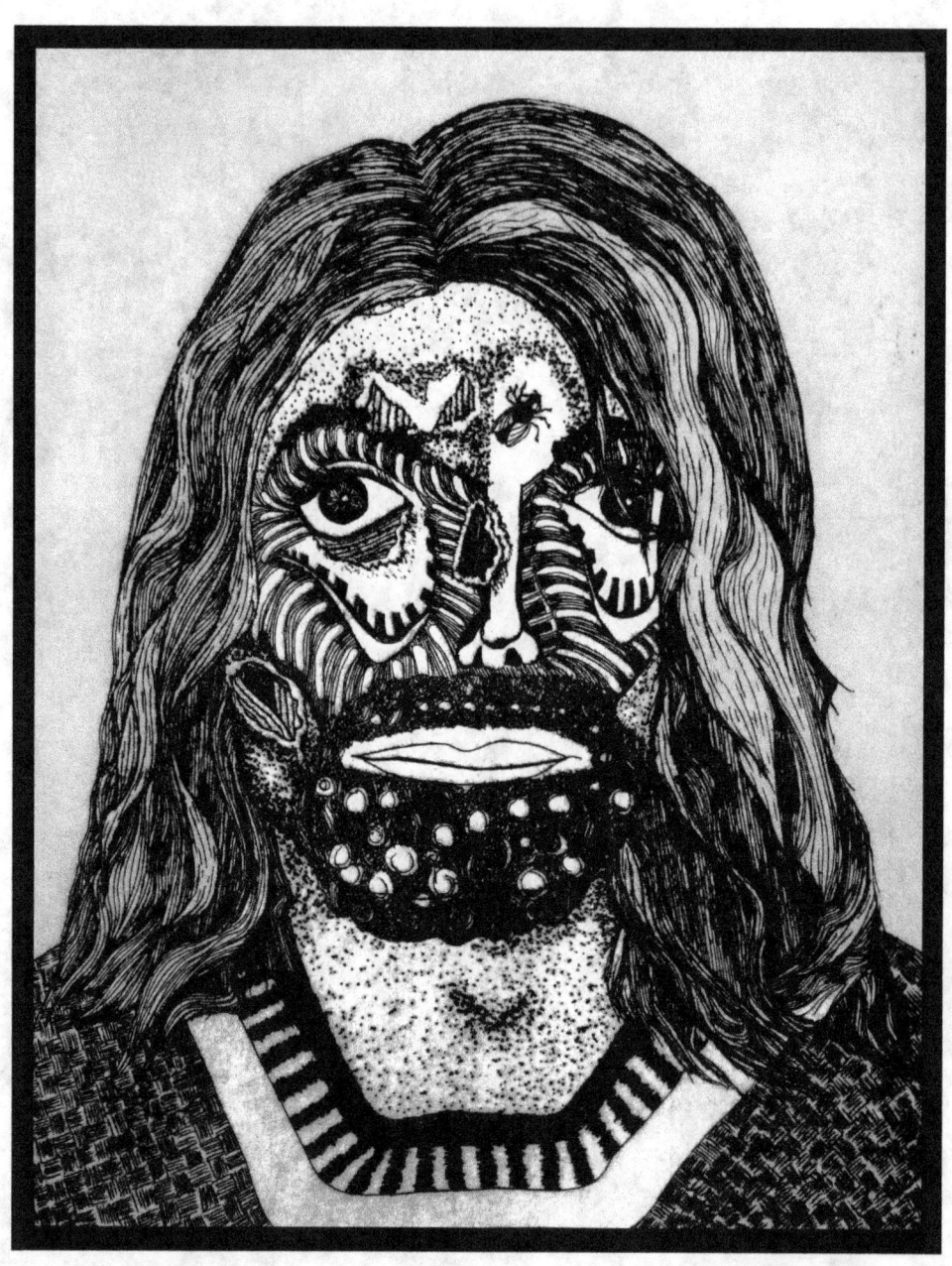

"SAID I NOT UNTO THEE, THAT, IF THOU WOULDEST BELIEVE, THOU
SHOULDEST SEE THE GLORY OF GOD?...AND WHEN HE THUS HAD
SPOKEN, HE CRIED WITH A LOUD VOICE, LAZARUS, COME FORTH.
AND HE THAT WAS DEAD CAME FORTH, BOUND HAND AND FOOT
WITH GRAVECLOTHES: AND HIS FACE WAS BOUND ABOUT WITH A
NAPKIN. JESUS SAITH UNTO THEM, LOOSE HIM, AND LET HIM GO."

- JOHN 11 : 40-44

FOR THE DAMNED...
...AND THE BAPTIZED.
Why I made this book and zombie evangelism...

I made this book for a few reasons... The first was to create a visual library of my mind's eye. All the drawings were done in permanent black and white pen, never erasing and never looking at other art, photos, or subjects for reference. It is an investigation on what visual cues have been engrained in my memory thus far. I also wanted to use the zombie and the grotesque as a tool for evangelism. I don't think this has been done thus far; it is my small contribution to the always growing field of zombies.

The most interesting evangelist I have ever heard was Brother Jed Smock. He is more of a performance artist than an evangelist. Jed tours around the United States preaching to insolent college students. Every year he makes a stop at the University of Minnesota; that is where I encounter him and search him out to hear his preaching. A typical Jed sermon involves screaming at masturbators, gays, fornicators, idolterers, frat boys, sorority girls, jews, moslims, and dissenting Christians. Jed is a gifted orator whose sermons often provoke fighting and public and pubic hetero and homosexual acts. Police are often called to watch. I personally have seen Jed bring scantily clad women to tears simply by screaming, "SLUT!" and pointing his menacing finger at them... wielding divine authority. I actually believe him when he claims that as a frat boy (when he was conveniently a sinner) he had such sexual prowess that he would seek out lesbians with which to fornicate and subsequently, "Straighten them out."

Jed is a character who has meshed evangelism with performance art. He is my tragic hero who has unfortunately and dangerously died and arisen more on the side of art rather than evangelism. Jed's flaw is that he will minimize Christian principles for the sake of performance and controversy. This book is my attempt to visually capture Jed's remarkable evangelical style, clinging to the line where evangelism crosses into art while hopefully avoiding dying and rising myself... into the pits of hell where there is grinding and gnashing of teeth.

Savor these 105 drawings; investigate them intensely and cautiously. Rather than a book with a story to decode, envision a series of 105 drawings, each able to stand on its own with its subtleties and contribution to the whole... Also keep in mind that I spent > 2 years drawing this.

With much love, effort, commitment, and passion I give you *Zombielzebub: Hell's Invasion!*

- John Frederick Beckmann, Ph.D. candidate

INTRODUCTION

John Steven Beckmann www.prairieuprising.com

SAEVO INDIGNATIO AND THE DANCE OF DEATH

Starkly linear graphics, the sharp incision of black into white, a
cycle of macabre and disturbing images: these phrases describe a
pictorial *genre*, the Dance of Death. The images in this portfolio
represent a *Totentanz*. The subject and form would be familiar to Hans
Holbein, Callot, Goya, and Otto Dix. Holbein the younger adapted the
medieval *Danse macabre*, often displayed in church frescos, to the new
medium of the graphic print in the first quarter of the 16th century. A
contemporary of Duerer, Holbein's engravings are sinister and satiric:
Death ambushes the living; a skeleton insinuates itself into a romantic
tryst, politicians and preachers pontificate to congregations that
include grinning death's heads. Callot's spidery mercenaries are cousin
to his uncanny, scrawny *Commedia dell' Arte* figures – they torture peas-
ants and murder one another with the grace of ballerinas or
praying mantises. Goya shows a world absurd with pretension and
idiotic with arrogance, slowly dissolving into assassination and rape.
Dix depicts war as the decomposition of spirit into rotting flesh. All of
these cycles of imagery, these dances of death, are moral works: they
castigate folly and pride by depicting its' inevitable outcome, death and
decay. (The grim black and white photographs of Joel-Peter Witkin
belong to this genre as well). I place John Fredrick Beckmann's
Zombielzebub: Hell's Invasion in this lineage. Beckmann's subject
matter may be spilt brains, exposed entrails and deliquescent flesh, but
his stony linear style petrifies his figures into dismaying allegories:
there is something austere and even classical about his monsters
chiseled into black and white as fiercely austere as Mantegna's saints
petrified in their postures of abasement and martyrdom.

The moral intent of these images is made manifest in the first narrative picture of the second portfolio. In a rocky desert where cacti stand like the trees of Golgotha, a great crane rises against the horizon. The construction crane takes the form of a mighty scale, standing in silhouette. The scale is the figure of justice. It reminds us of the Egyptian *Book of the Dead*, a text illustrating the judgement of the dead at the scale of Ma'at. In early Egyptian mythology, death was followed by immediate judgement. Anubis, the hyena-headed psychopomp, conveyed the zombie-like dead person into a hall of judgment – there the corpse's heart was weighed on a scale to determine it's quanta of righteousness. The virtuous dead were invited into heaven's banqueting halls; the wicked were tossed into an inferno to be devoured by Ammut. Ammut was a monster worthy of Beckmann's most visionary imagery: a huge beast with the maw of a crocodile, the body of a lion, and the hindquarters of a hippopotamus. Mythology is philosophy in its primal form. Accordingly, myth is rationalized into philosophy and vaporized into theology. In later Egyptian practice, the judgment of the dead man's heart developed into a theatrical legal process involving a panoply of gods. Anubis led the dead man into the Hall of Ma'at where Osiris presided over a kind of trial: the dead man's heart was weighed against a feather, presumably from an ostrich. Thoth, the god of writing, served as a stenographer, a kind of ibis-skulled stenographer. If the dead man's heart weighed more than a feather on the scale of justice, the deceased was hurled into the pit of Ammut. By the period of the Ptolemaic pharaohs, when Egypt was Alexandrian and, therefore, Greek, Ma'at became identified with the *Logos* – that is the principal of linguistic, that is, grammatical, order in the universe. This foray into comparative mythology is an elaborate way of saying that Beckmann's portfolio depicts a judgment day, an apocalypse, the final hour in which the living and the dead are judged. Indeed, Beckmann shows us the *logos* on the first page of his picture-cycle, the figure of the word made flesh, Jesus – savior but depicted in a curious manner. (We will have more to say about the *logos* later). Beckmann's Jesus is both a clown, the Jester of God, and some sort of cosmology. I am un-decided whether the whorls of black and white from which the figure is comprised represent a clown's make-up or the landscape of nebula and supernova in deep space. It is clear that his brow is festooned with an insect – kin to the dung-beetle that we see in the infernal pit excavated in the desert in the second portfolio. (The dung-beetle, of course, is also a symbol in Egyptian mythology, an image for Ra, another supreme and judgmental God, the embodiment of the sun, conceived in the form of the beetle rolling its pellet of offal across the stony desert). And what is the mark at the top of Christ's sternum – is it just a shadow reflecting a depression in the figure or the mark of a tracheotomy?

Various narratives can be construed from the portfolios of images. The second group of pictures called "Ancient Burial Tombs" almost tells a story: the scales of Justice is a crane towering over an immense open pit mine. These works, like Dante's hell, consist of concentric rings where trucks labor ascending and descending the pit's sheer walls. The place seems built with spiraling ramps like the Guggenheim. Two workers seem to have uncovered an artifact. At the tip of their shovels, a black scarab, apparently embossed in bronze or stone makes a navel in the pit's center. Further excavation reveals that the scarab is a tiny keyhole-like decoration adorning a large intricate gateway bearing hieroglyphs and sinister designs. The foreman, or, perhaps, job superintendent has come to view the discovery. A striking image gives us a close-up of his skeletal face, opaque sunglasses, jaws agape in a toothy grimace. Why does the boss wear a scarab ornament identical to the insect marking the hell-gate? Is the point of the excavation to uncover this opening into some other world? We never find out: lumpy naked zombies, with rotting entrails in cages of rib, appear from nowhere and devour our characters. Crucial to the sequence of images are two matching hell-mouths – the gate with its morbid decorations and the boss' cadaverous maw. If you seek hell, you will find it. And with predictably dire consequences. Herculean effort ends with zombies eating your flesh. The remaining portfolios exemplify this theme: a general sets forth to war, commanding tanks and troops. But the battlefield suddenly swarms with rats (and more lumpish looking walking corpses) and everyone is eaten alive. The general's counterpart is a zombie commander who wears a crown: Death is the king of the battlefield. In "Science", the artist portrays himself and not in a flattering light. Looking puerile and nervous, the artist is dressed in a lab smock. He is accompanied by a mannish woman wearing a badge "Graduate Student Bitch". Inexplicably, scientists are toting around a cage containing a mutilated animal, possibly some sort of half-decayed dog. The dog's corpse seems to mutate into a peculiar bloated body, apparently female. We realize that the dog, probably female and, therefore, (like the graduate student) a bitch, somehow relates to woman's corpse – the corpse is pregnant with death, the dead woman's belly is swollen, although this seems to be post-mortem bloating. (Beckmann's draftsmanship is sometimes unclear: I am informed that the animal that I perceived as a dog is, in fact, a rat, the maternal undead rat that has spawned the legions of zombie rodents devouring the tank and the other instruments of war in other images in this series. The exact species of Beckmann's monstrosities may evade characterization – it suffices to say that they are dead things obscurely animate with hatred for the living.) The artist as scientist and his colleague have captured some zombies for study – they are researching the nature and etiology of the zombie phenomenon. The protagonists dissect the woman's corpse and extract some nameless substance. The scientist deploys the "graduate bitch" both as dynamo (she powers the scanning electron microscope by peddling a bicycle apparatus) and some kind of bellows – her puffing into the microscope echoes the theme of bloating that motivates this picture sequence. Whatever the scientist-artist has discovered, it turns out to be valuable: our hero appears on TV and, apparently, founds a corporation devoted to zombie research. In the next section, "Hippies," the undead participate in an orgy. A phallic guitar presides over the festivities which include much oral copulation. Apparently, the zombies have been become politically active – they protest anti-abortion laws which, to their way of thinking, are anti-death. The artist-as-scientist is ambushed and devoured. In the next sequence, not content with rampaging across the earth, the undead take to outer space and attack astronauts. The whole cycle of drawings concludes with a *tour-de-force*, "The Rite". In these pictures, Albrecht Duerer's influence – particularly his illustrations to *Revelations* – is clear. (We have seen a previous citation to Duerer's woodcut of the martyrdom of the 11,000 virgins – in the background of one picture, we see zombies driving a mob of people off a high cliff, the picture mimicking the German artist's staging of that atrocity). "The Rite" seems to concern some kind of exorcism attempted by Catholic clergy. The artist's imagery seems anti-Papist, presumably deriving from the penny-dreadful woodcuts made during the Reformation by fanatical Lutherans. The priests fail and zombies devour them, but, then, Christ appears, a machine gun in his mouth (like Duerer's God tongued with a huge sword in the Apocalypse) and hell on earth is harrowed: perhaps, Jesus defeats the zombies, although the outcome is unclear.

W. H. Auden wrote: *Nobody is ever sent to Hell. He (or she) insists on going there.*

Beckmann's art is ugly. His draftsmanship is uncertain. Many of the figures are grotesquely twisted and bent. Postures and gesture are resolutely non-anatomical. It is unclear whether this is intentional or a defect in his art. In any event, the clumsiness of much of his draftsmanship only increases the cumulative power of the picture cycle – his figures are like the doll-like stick figures that populate the visionary etchings of James Ensor. They are less figures than citations of figures, not pictures but signs. Monsters swarm the images, filling the graphic frame to bursting. Reading the pictures requires decoding – that is, disentangling in one's imagination knots and intestinal whorls of interlocked figures. Beckmann seems to have a *horror vacui* – most of the images are intensely *worked*, textured with stippling or obsessively incised parallel lines. Curiously, several of his most effective pictures are those with the least minutely fashioned texturing. In particular, there is an image of shotgun blast scattering a zombie into a nebula of exploding flesh. Where there is no exploding flesh and no explosive gunburst, the image is blank – and all the more powerful for incorporating empty space into the picture. The art is a species of caricature. Again: Auden is very good on caricature:

> *We indulge in caricature with respect to our friends because*
> *we want to portray as they will always be to us. With regard*
> *to our enemies, we use caricature because it resists the notion*
> *that they will change and that we will have to forgive them.*

Is it permissible to wish that Beckmann had devoted his considerable talents to some subject less macabre and horrific? Gazing at a wall festooned with these images, the viewer is overwhelmed by their fetishistic excess, their obsessive single-mindedness, their grim and overt sadism. The viewer's response is bemused: *Why?* But, of course, all art that is not purely mercantile raises this same question. Except for a few titans – Courbet, Rembrandt, Duerer, and Picasso come to mind – artists always specialize in a certain trade-mark subject matter. We can forgive Goya for his war-disasters, perhaps, and the wild, dark fantasy of his *Caprichos*, but what about the 33 etchings with aquatint comprising that artist's *Tauromachia*. Wouldn't it be better for the world if one of Goya's greatest last works *wasn't* about bullfighting but something more politically or aesthetically correct? Aren't the acres of obese female flesh lovingly painted by Rubens or the elderly Renoir just a little bit embarrassing? Indeed, even the realm of beauty can seem oppressive: does Frangonard have to be so meticulously luscious in the erotic scenes that he obsessively paints again and again. My point, I suppose, is an inevitable one, but worth stating explicitly – an artist is entitled to his obsessions and to make the pictures that seem important to him. We may wish Constable, another great master at portraying slime, rot, and decay, had devoted his magisterial skills to painting battlefields after the manner of Gros or David, but he didn't, and he couldn't, that subject was beyond his expressive register. Ultimately, the image is as closely rooted in the quiddity of the artist's imagination as the word *image* is embedded in *imagination*. And, in any event, when we criticize an artist's choice of subject matter, we always misunderstand, to a certain extent, what has driven that artist to embody his ideas in his choice of imagery. I'm sure Beckmann's zombies and moldering corpses represent something to the artist that is not merely spectral and ugly. Something, we sense, underlies this imagery and translates its morbidity into a realm of significance that we can intuit, but not fully comprehend. After writing this essay, I spoke with Beckmann briefly about my interpretation of his work. The artist assured me with easy confidence *that not one single thing that I had written was in any way true to his motives or intents*. I had misread every image. Thus: *caveat lector!*

Figurative art, like Gaul, occupies three provinces: history, the nude, and the pastoral. Landscapes are pastoral and the domain of the beautiful. All figure drawing, including portrait painting, is a category of the nude. Recall that Eakins insisted that his students study anatomy, even though, perhaps, their *metier* would be society portraits. Every clothed figure is naked underneath. The practice of the great painters of the renaissance was similar: musculature, even if draped, was decisive. The nude is the domain of the true: portraits, whether naked or clothed, aim at disclosure and revelation. History is the domain of memory. But history painting is also a species of rhetoric, *laus et vituperatio*, praise and blame in a political sense. Beckmann's images are forms of history painting, Swiftian rhetorical exercises in blame. Praise (*laus*) arises only in the last portfolio. In "The Rite," the images achieve something approaching the sublime – defined as a mixture of terror and coercive beauty. In "The Rite," the undead occupy the earth. They no longer have anyone to attack. Everyone, it seems, has succumbed except a set of heretical knights of the faith who are, perhaps, as wicked as the zombies that they battle. Several images, worthy of Brueghel and Bosch, show the world in flames with zombies cruising the streets in cars or driving great iron-wheeled carts over cadavers. A zombie wearing an elaborate ecclesiastical crown appears in an image designed to look like a coat of arms – the undead are sovereign. Wielding severed heads like the mysterious Baphomet of the Knights Templar, a group of armored avengers gather. It appears that our artist has included a self-portrait among their number. Some sort of religious ritual occurs. Then, a startlingly symmetrical drawing shows us three figures clad in vestments dismembering a zombie. The figures are monstrous, but somehow beautiful: one has the head of an eagle, another is lion-headed, the third gripping a blade in its teeth is a winged oxen. Immediately, we understand that we are in presence of the Evangelists. Mark, Luke, and John are portrayed in apocalyptic imagery in the form of a lion, a bull, and an eagle. I suspect that Beckmann's imagery is inaccurate: I presume the three beast-headed angels that he portrays are meant to be Mark, Luke, and Matthew. John is the artist and, as we will see, he makes a spectacular appearance in the pictures following the advent of the three evangelists on this apocalyptic scene. (Traditionally, Matthew is portrayed as a winged human figure – however, in Beckmann's apocalypse, John, the artist, the human avatar of the apocalypse). The bull and eagle bear swords between their teeth – the Word or *Logos* is, at once, gospel and sword of righteousness cleaving the wicked from the just. Several horrific Catholic priests pour fluid from a jug containing a human head down John's throat. He arises, dressed in vestments and wearing a Cardinal's cap that bears the crossed keys of the Papacy. Clearly, the picture cycle is intended to represent a fourth Gospel, the Gospel of the artist John Frederick Beckmann. A mighty sword extends like a tusk from his mouth. The final two images in the portfolio are the most grandiose: in one Jesus, himself, like Samson, rends apart the jaws of one of the monsters drawing the iron-wheeled cart of the Apocalypse. In the last image, an enigmatic figure with long parted hair and surrounded by a glory of light, sweeps across the picture. The figure is clearly not Christ – beneath the image, a banner whips and twists bearing the artist's initials. The *Logos* has here become a submachine gun protruding from the Avenger's mouth. This destroying angel is heavily armed; he wears a garland of hand grenades and clutches another machine gun that he fires into the crowned Zombie. For the time being, it seems, that some species of the divine has prevailed.

Jan. 3rd 2011

Zombielzebub

Hell's Invasion

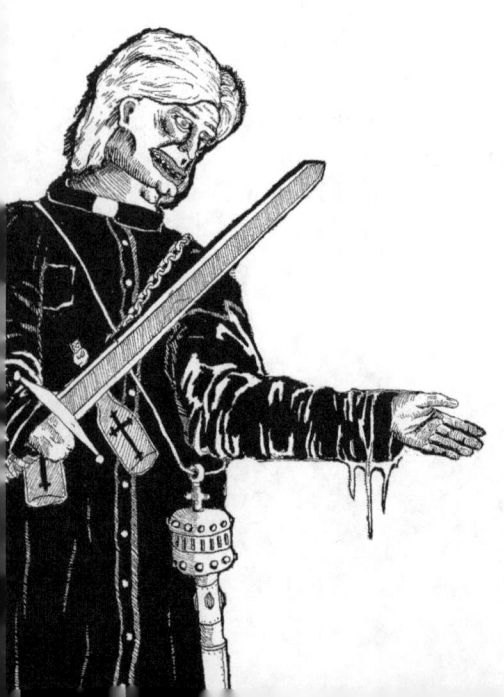

~~Portfolio 1~~

~~Normal life~~

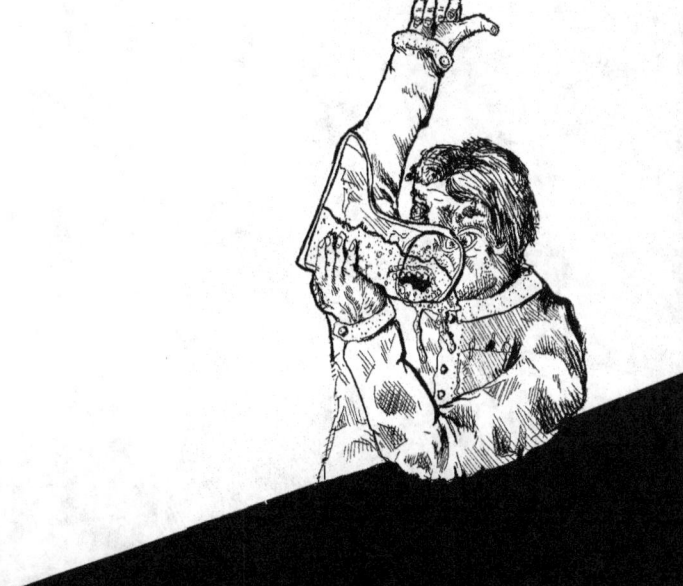

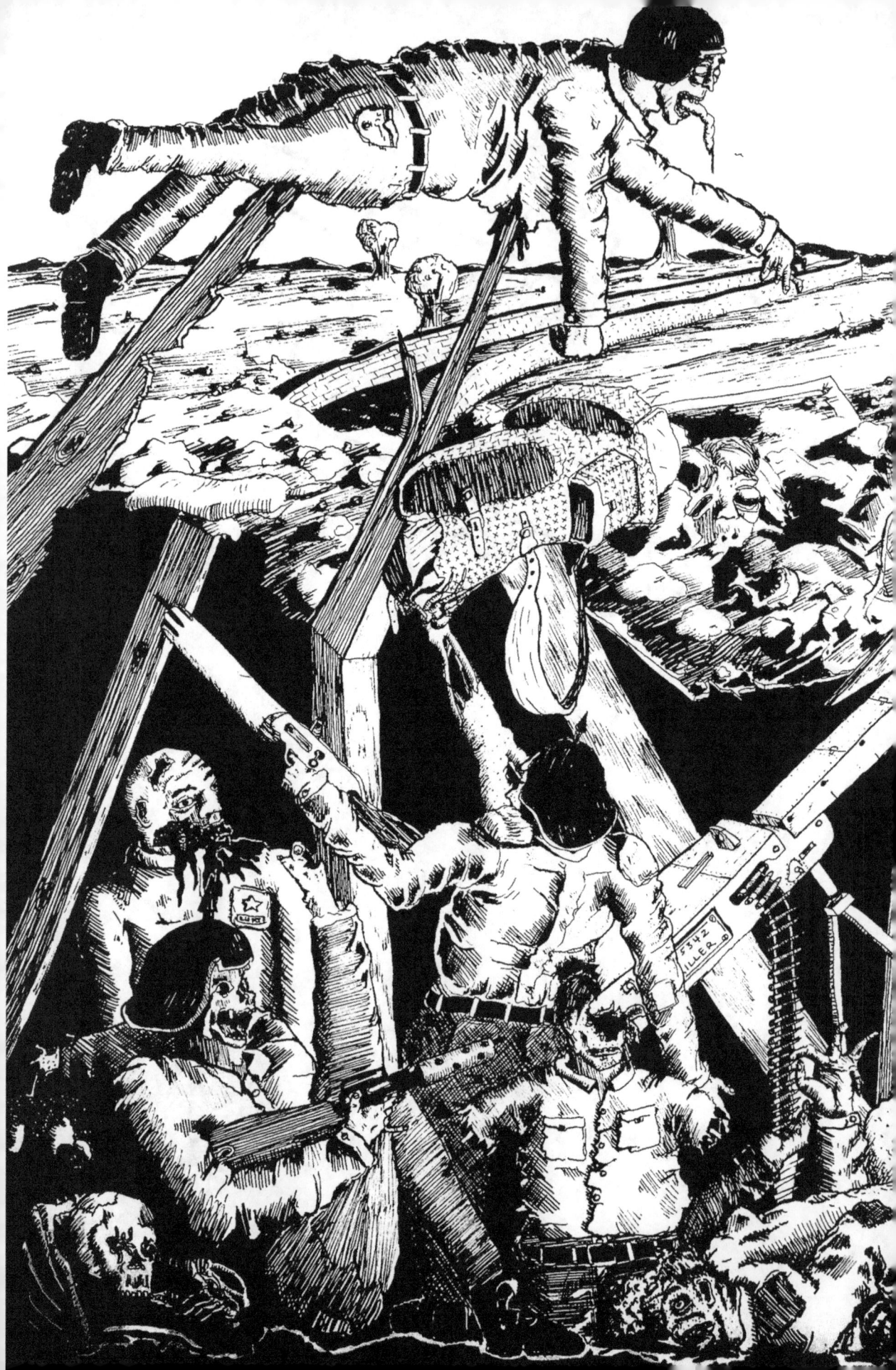

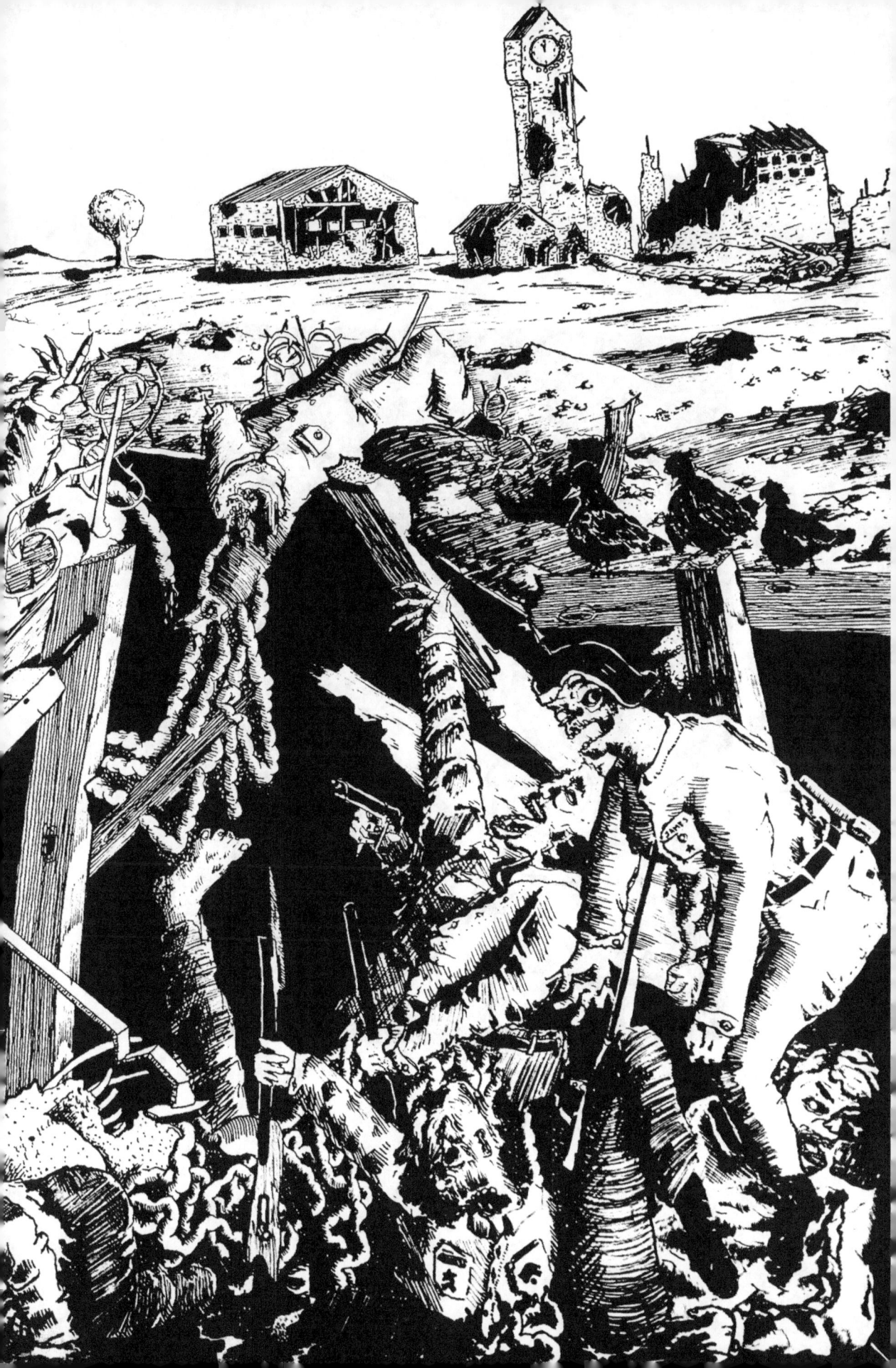

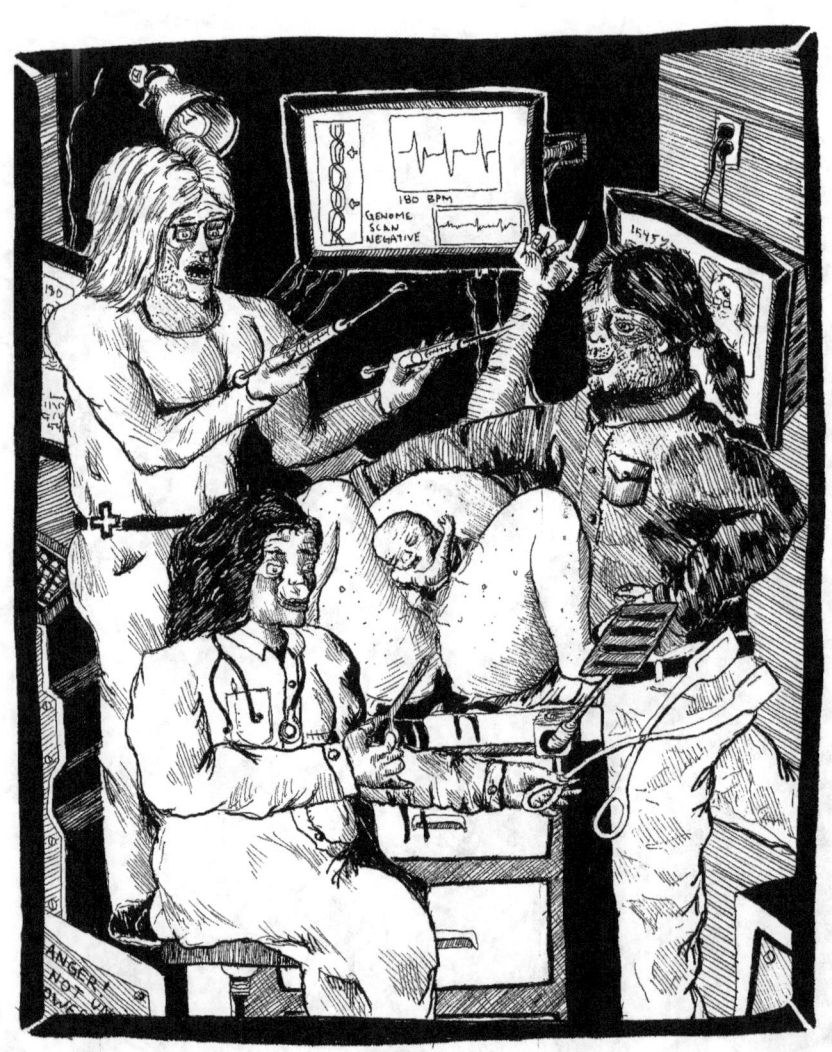

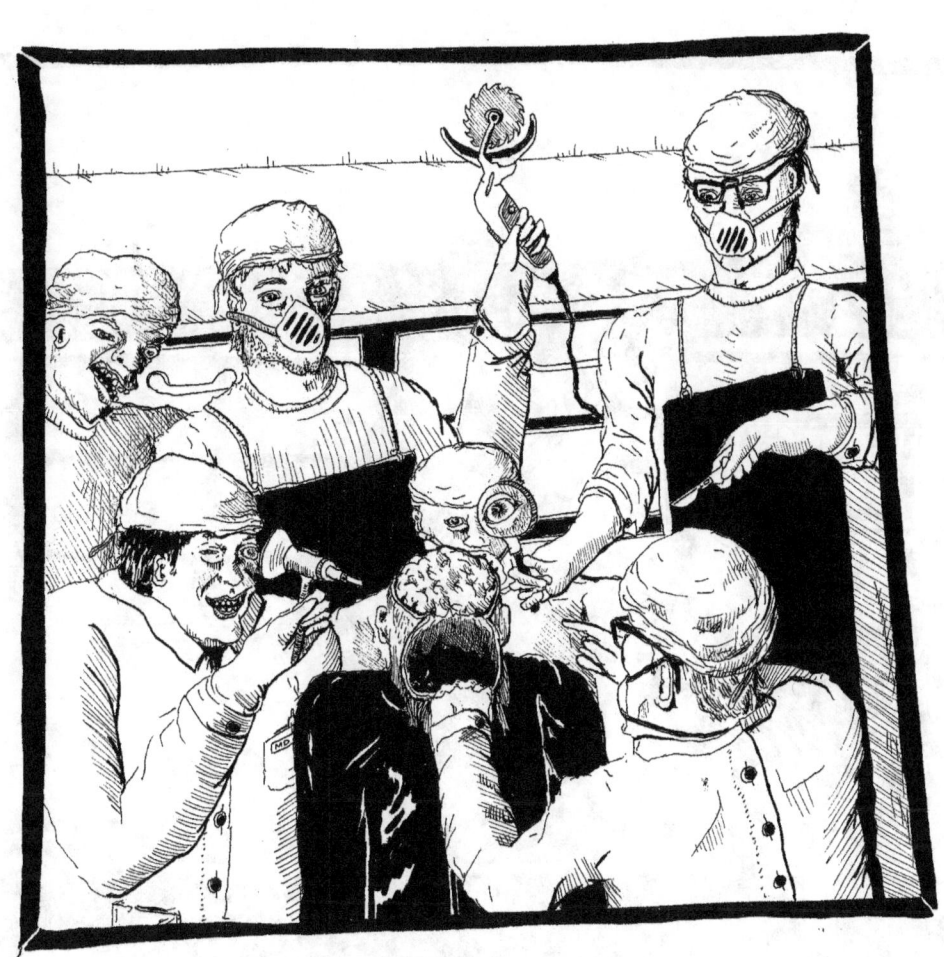

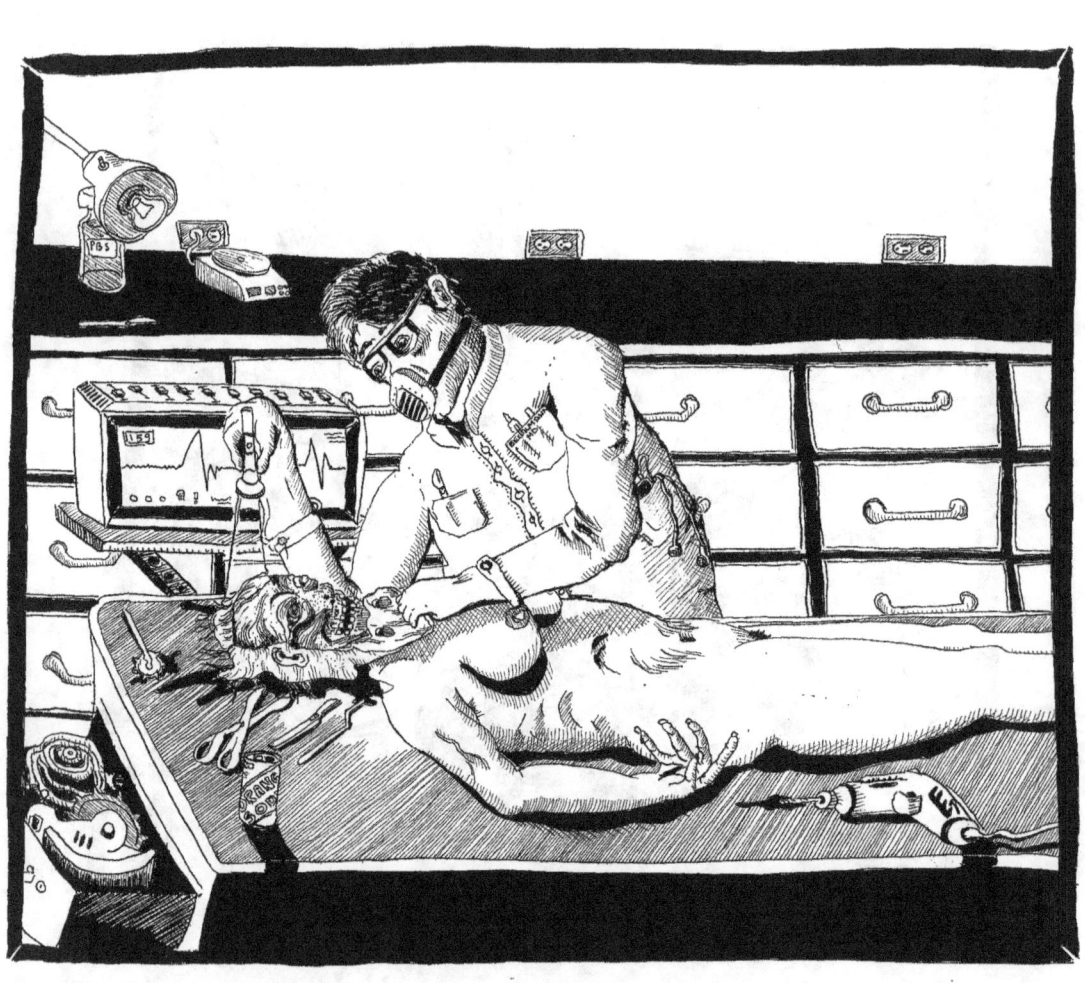

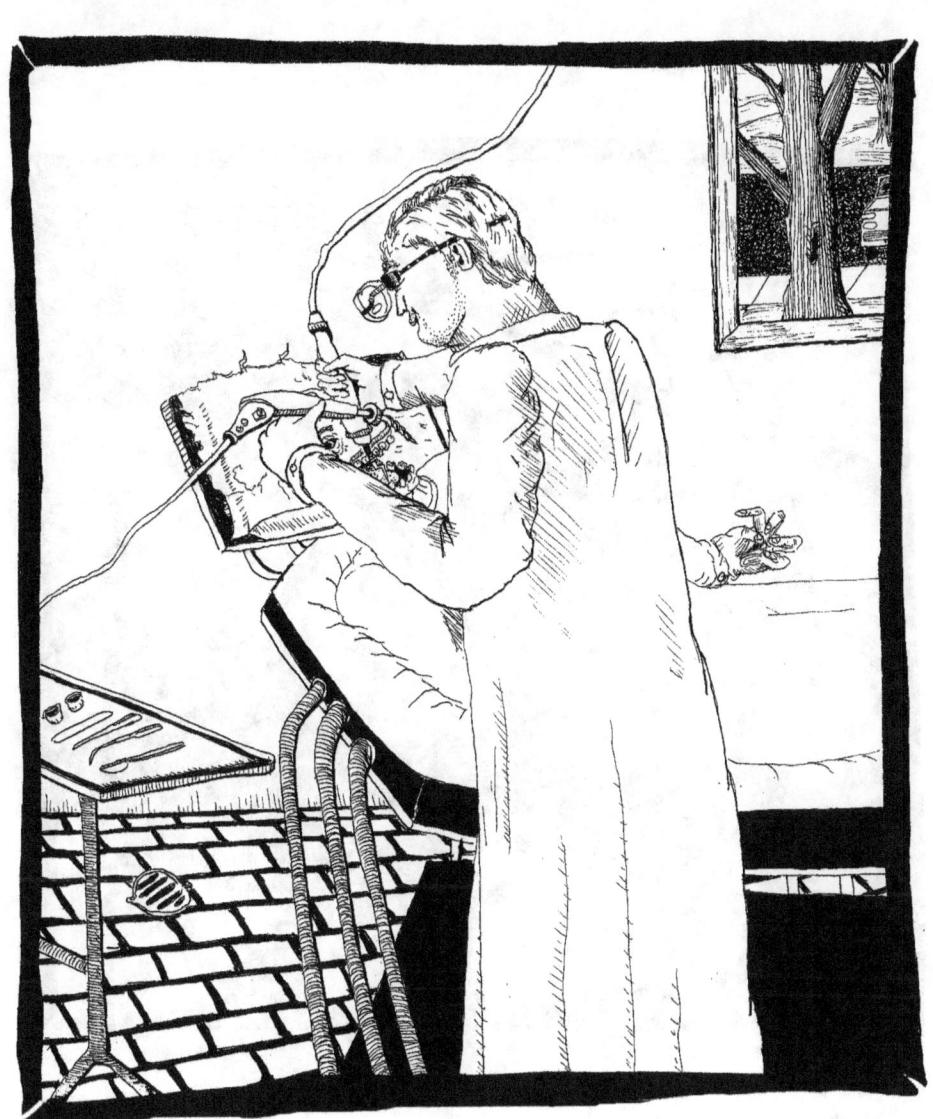

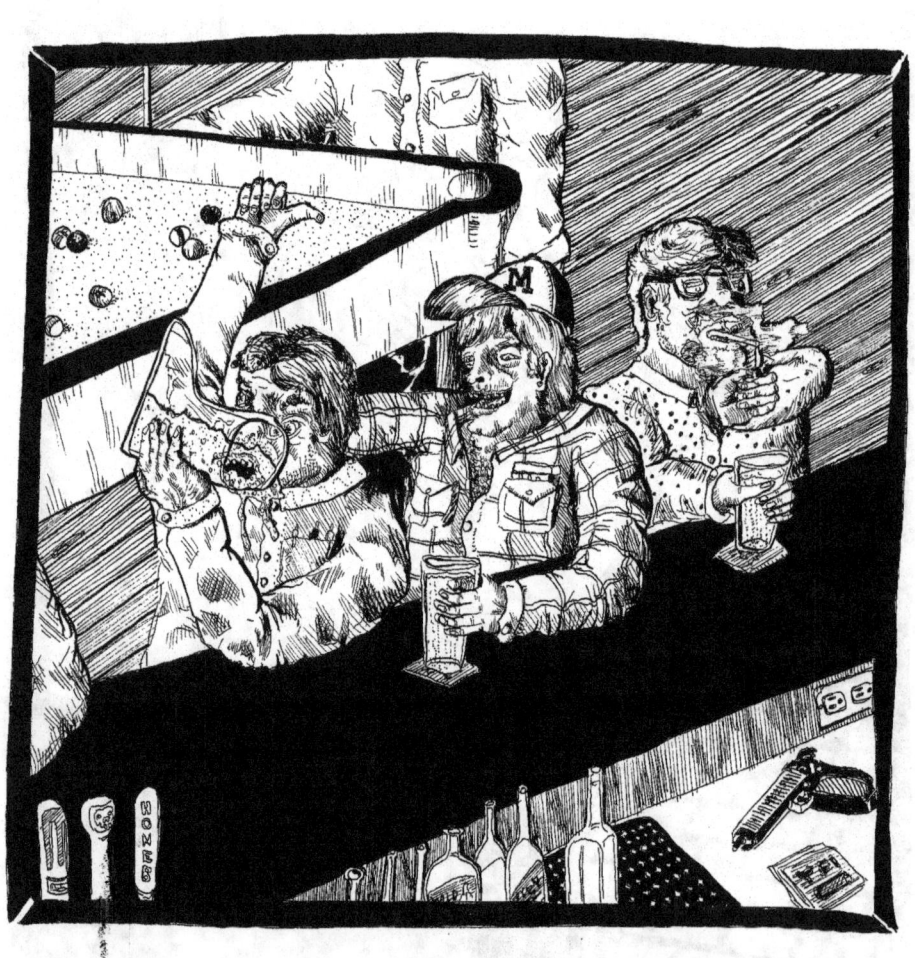

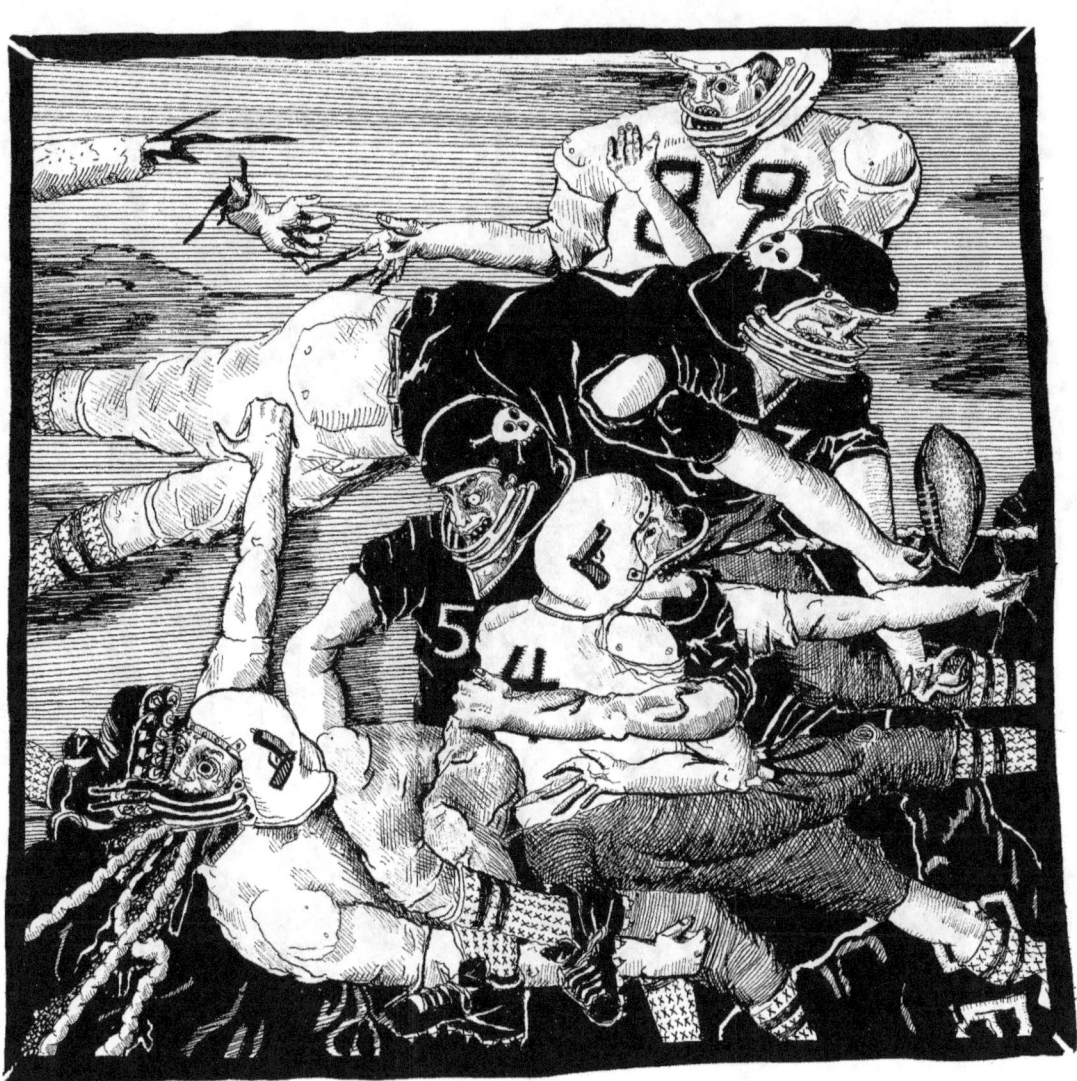

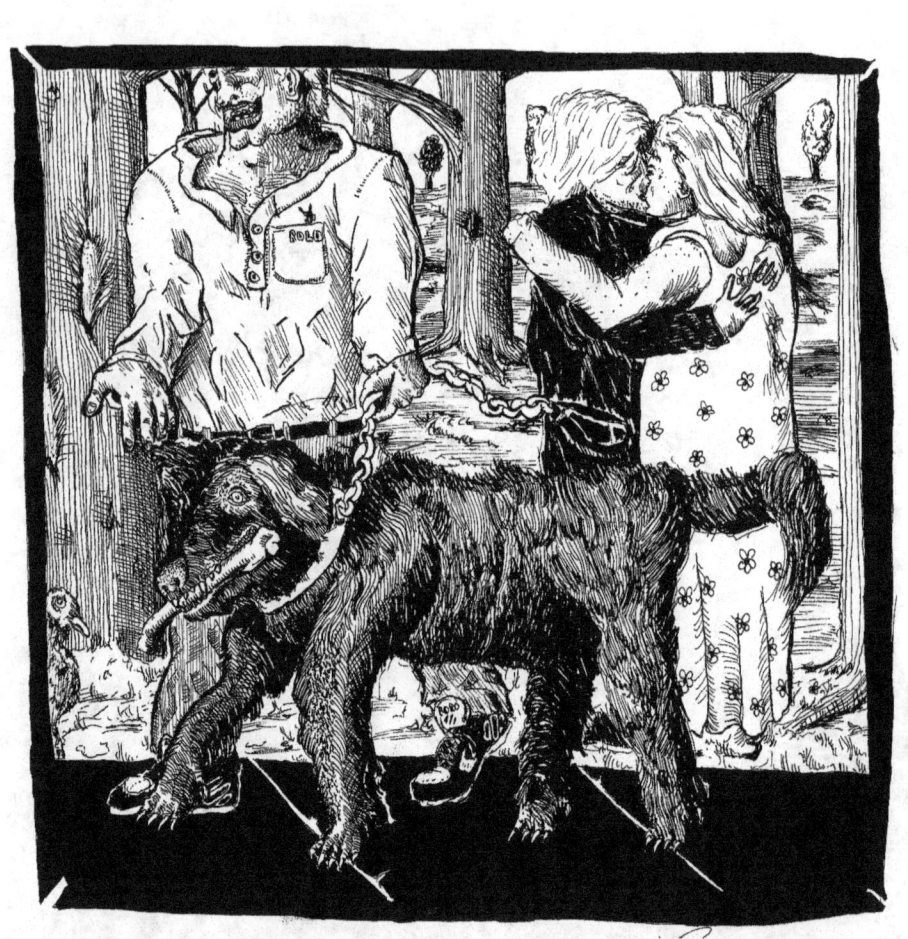

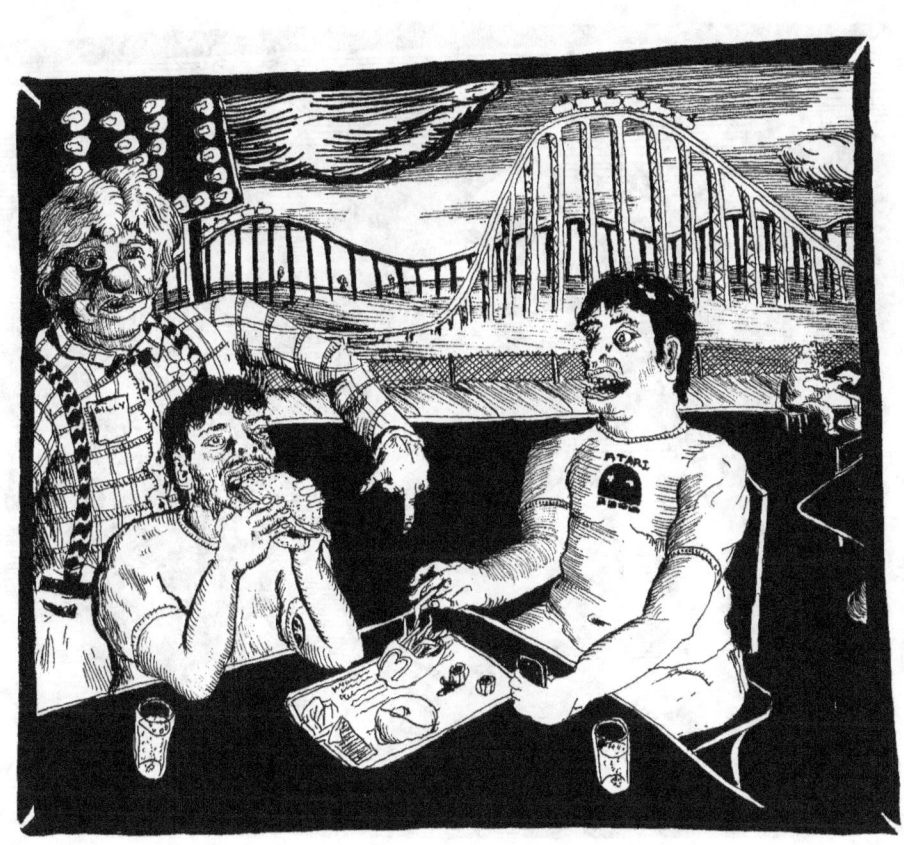

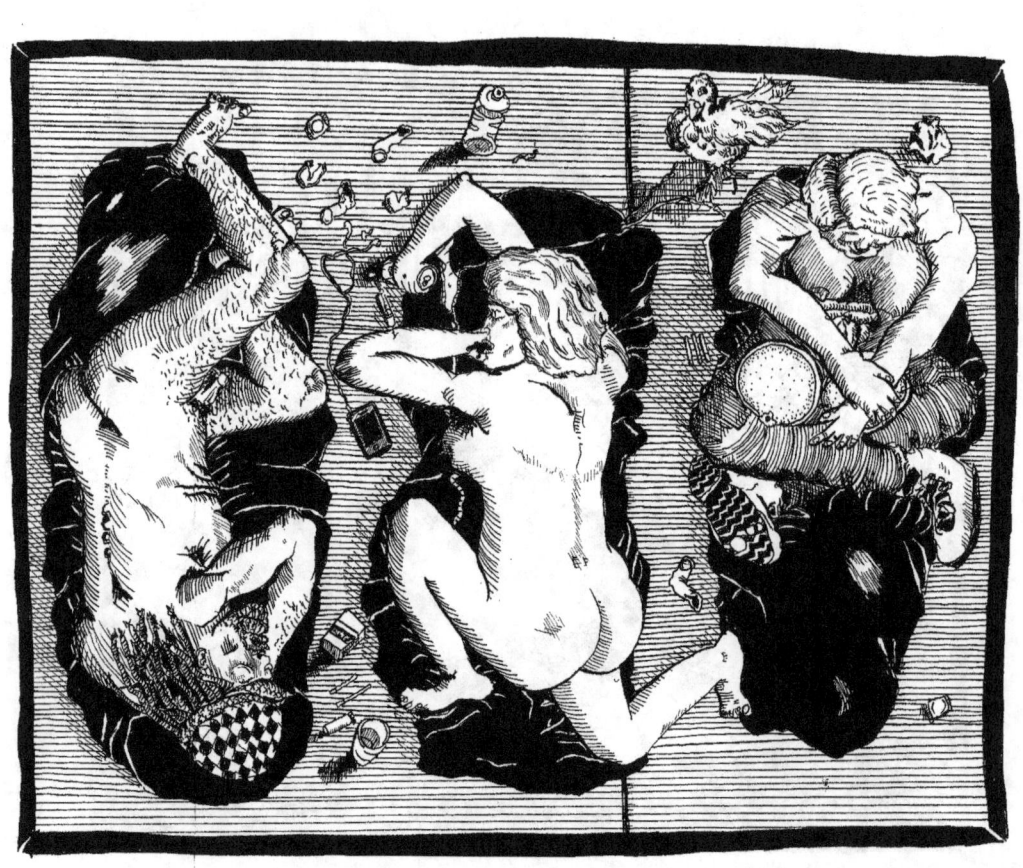

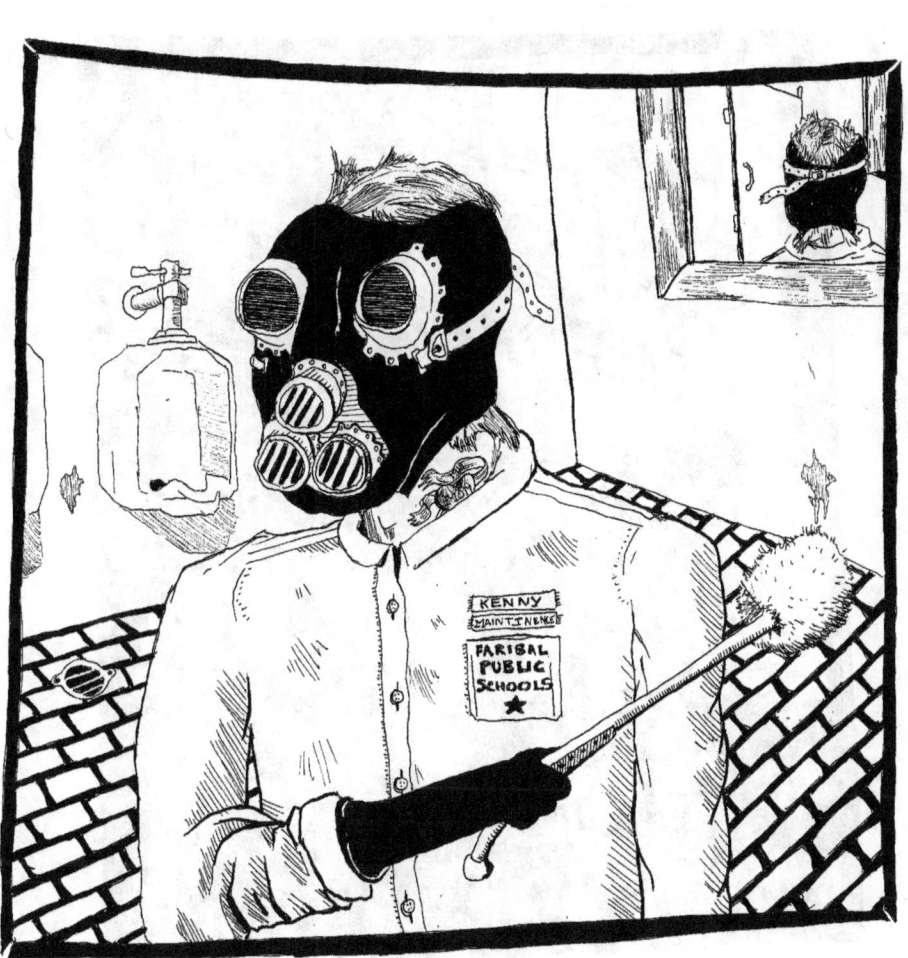

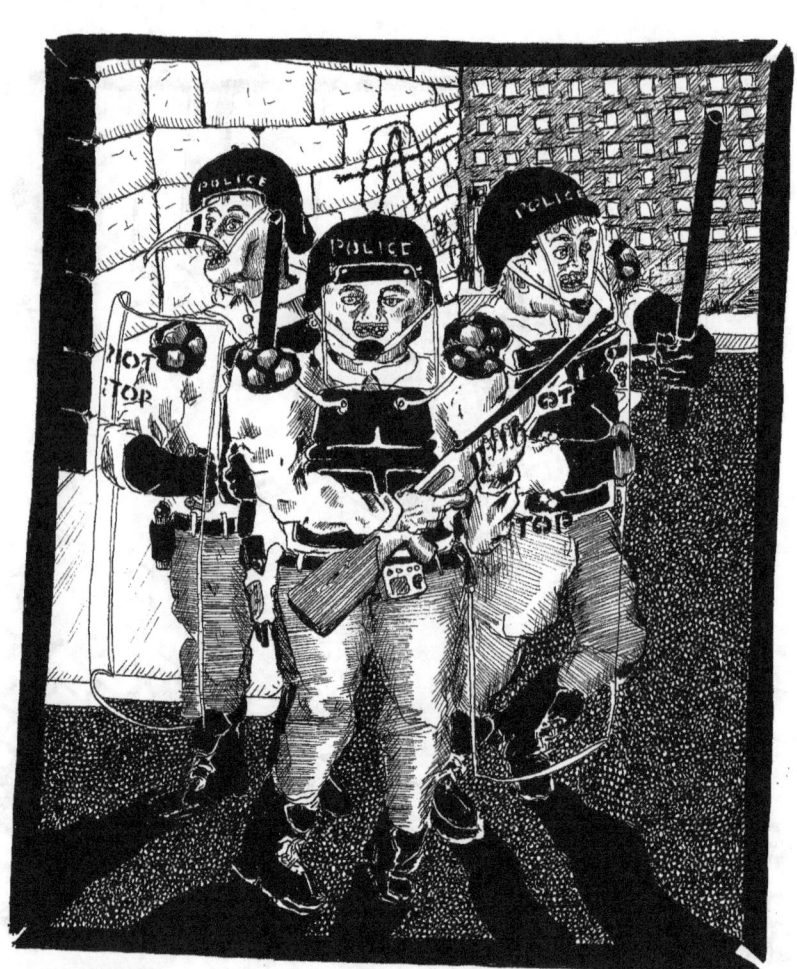

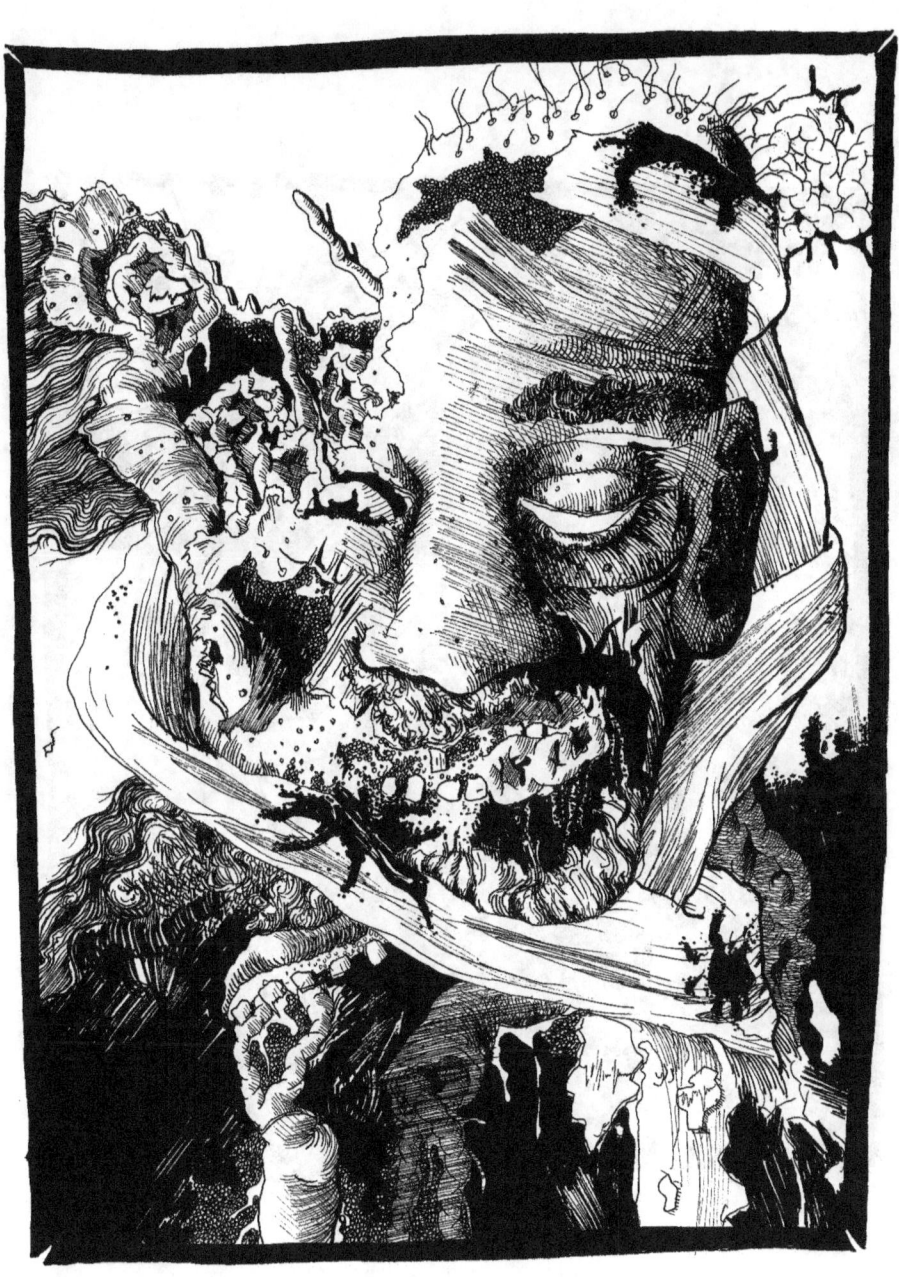

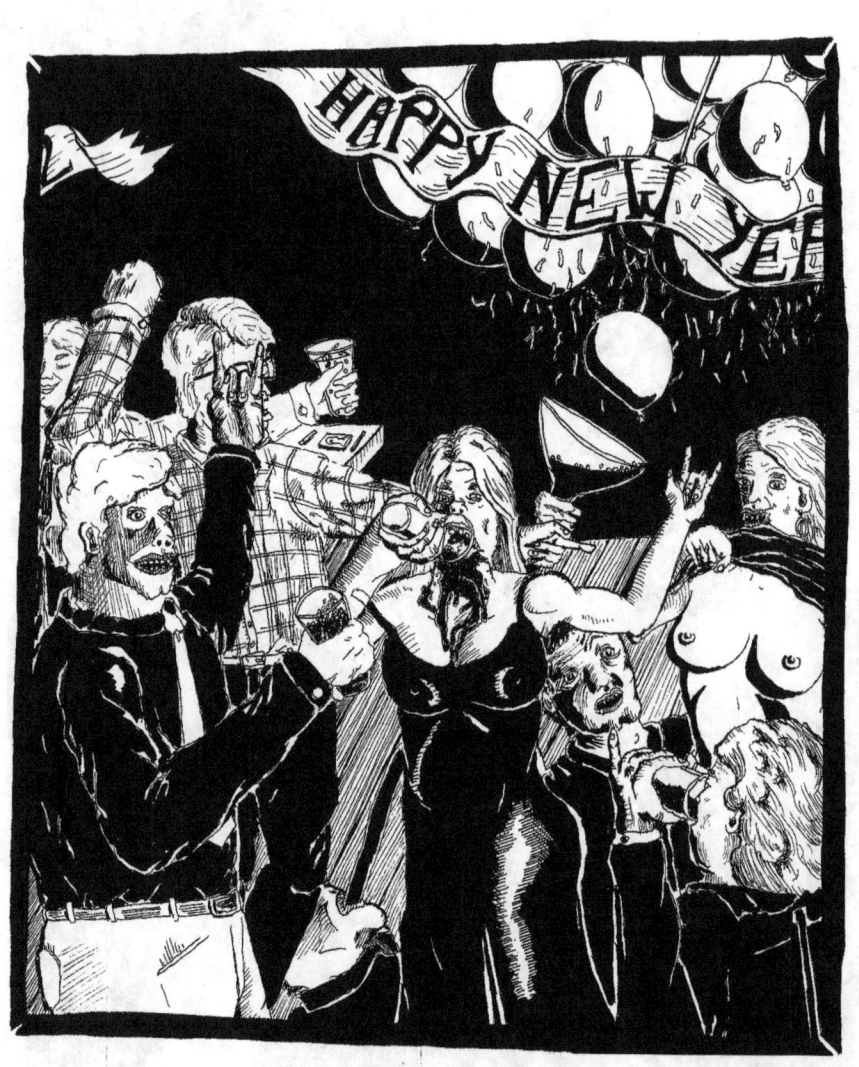

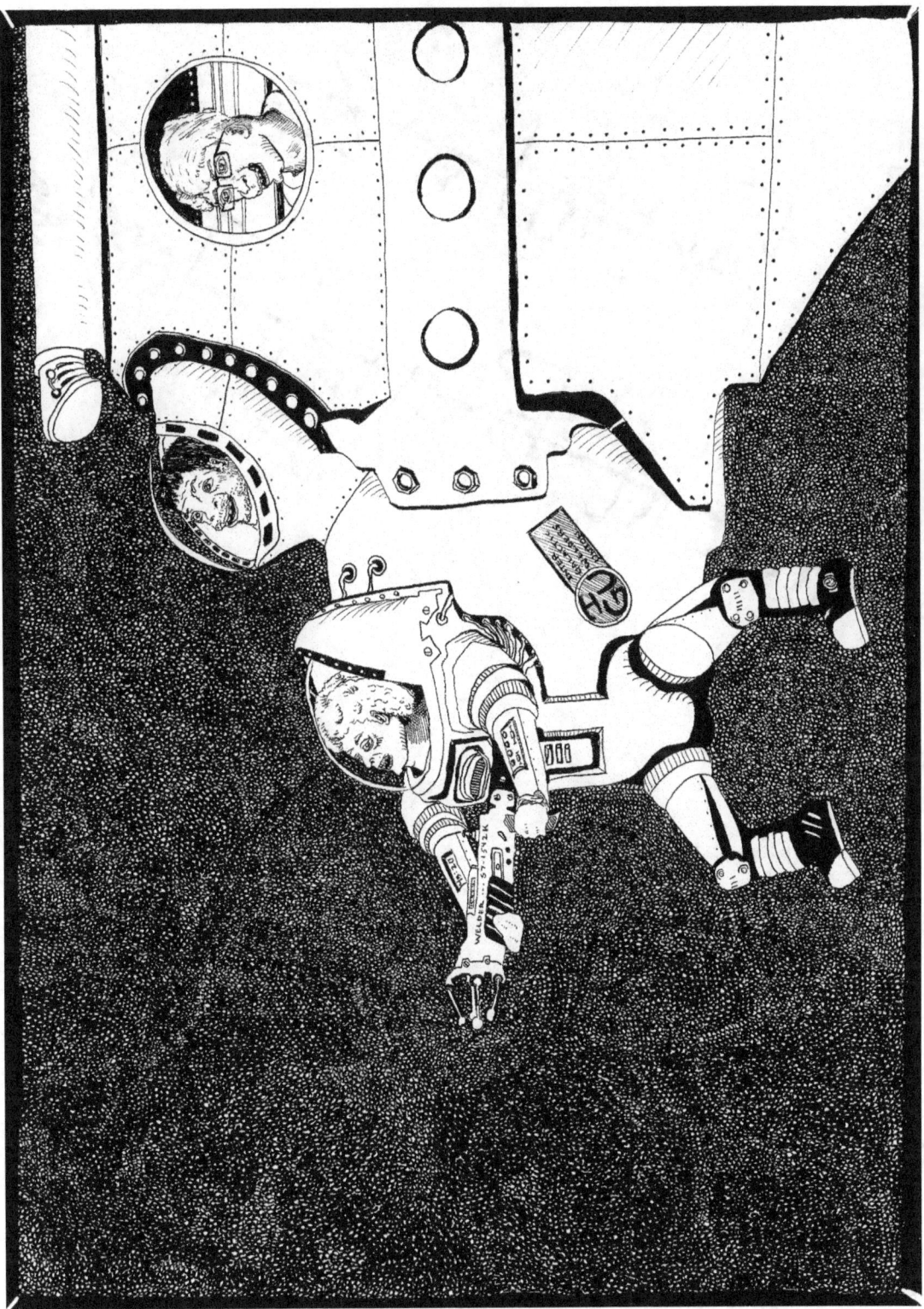

Portfolio 2
Ancient Burial Tombs

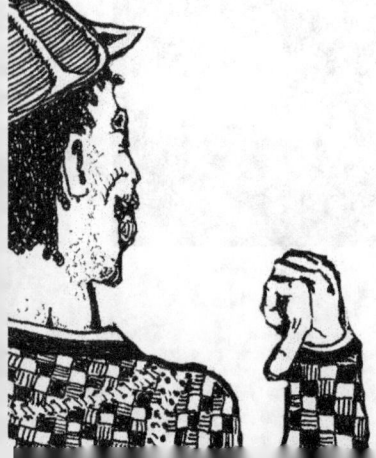

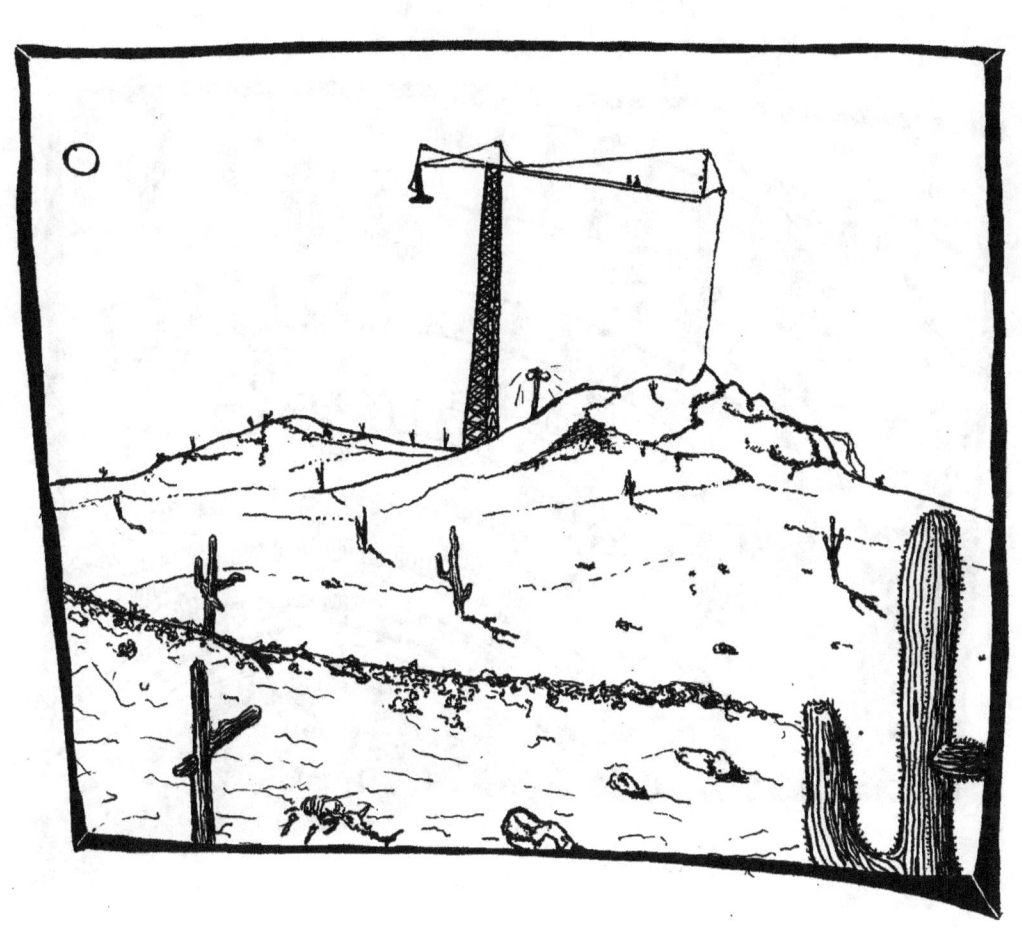

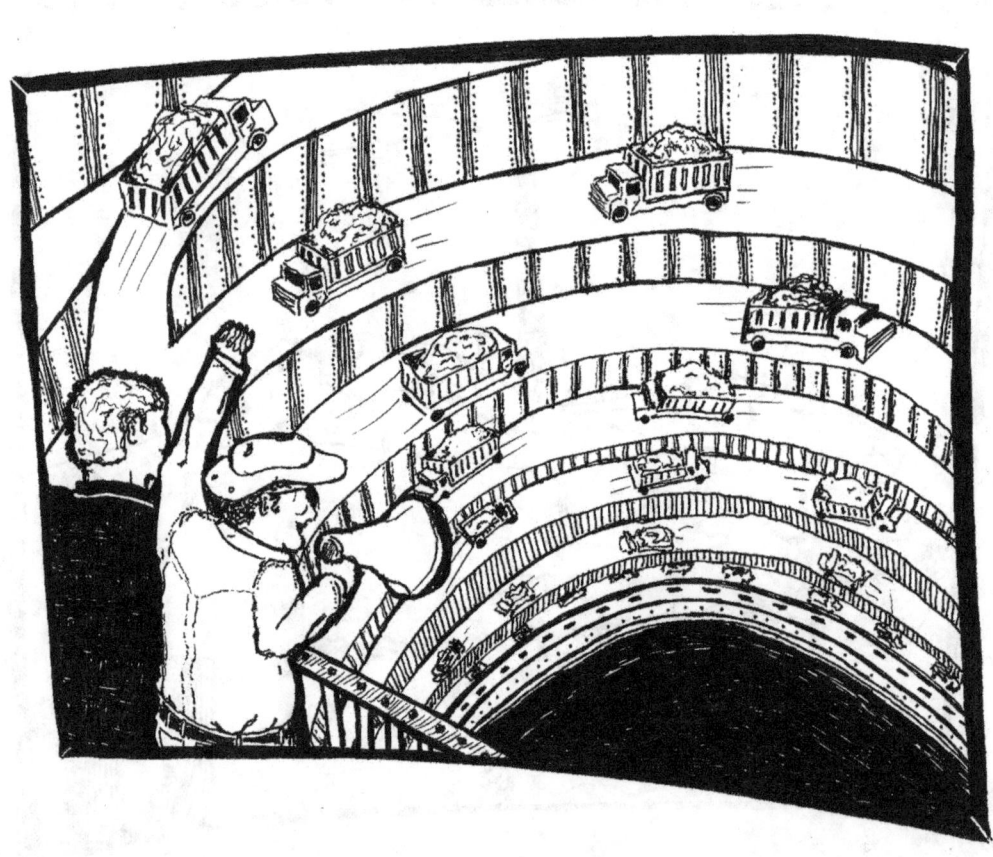

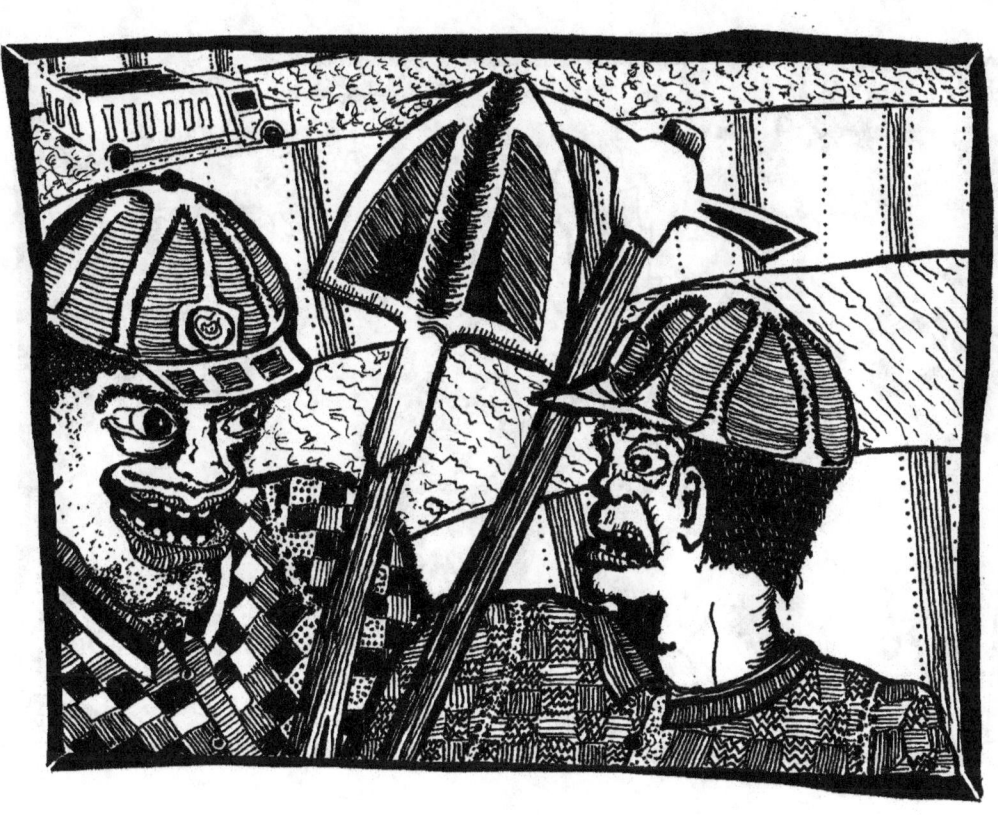

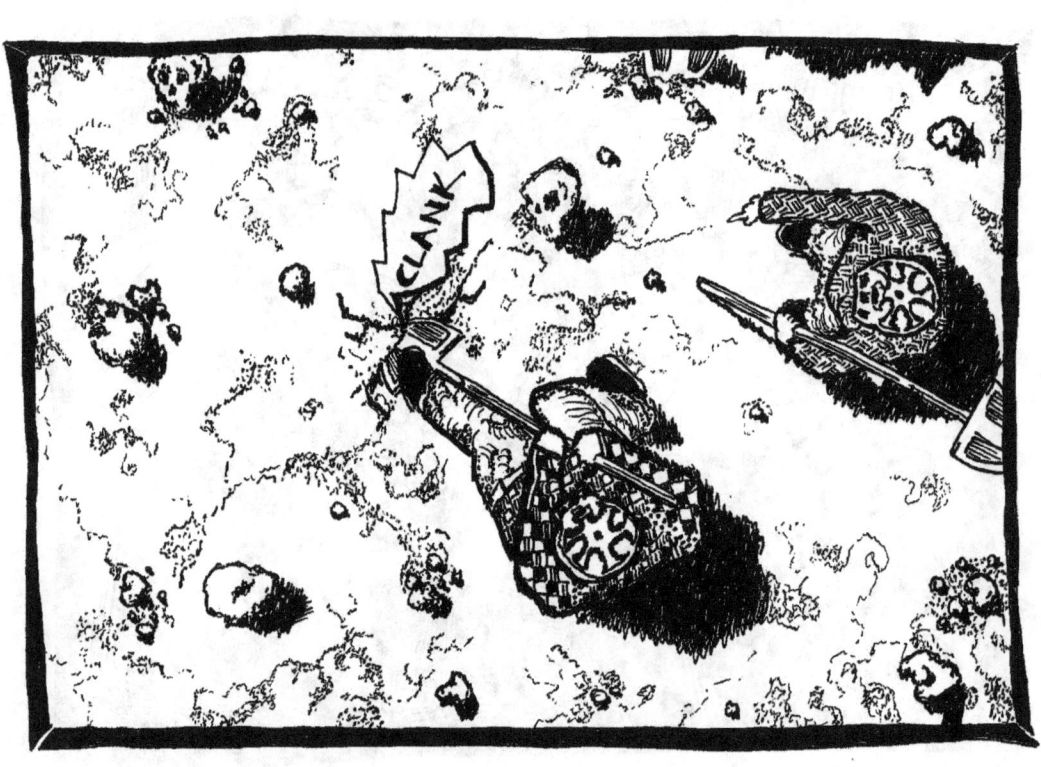

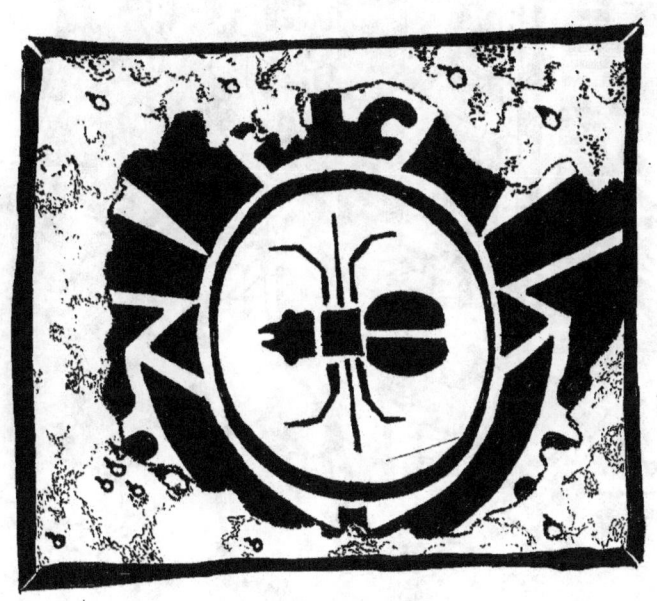

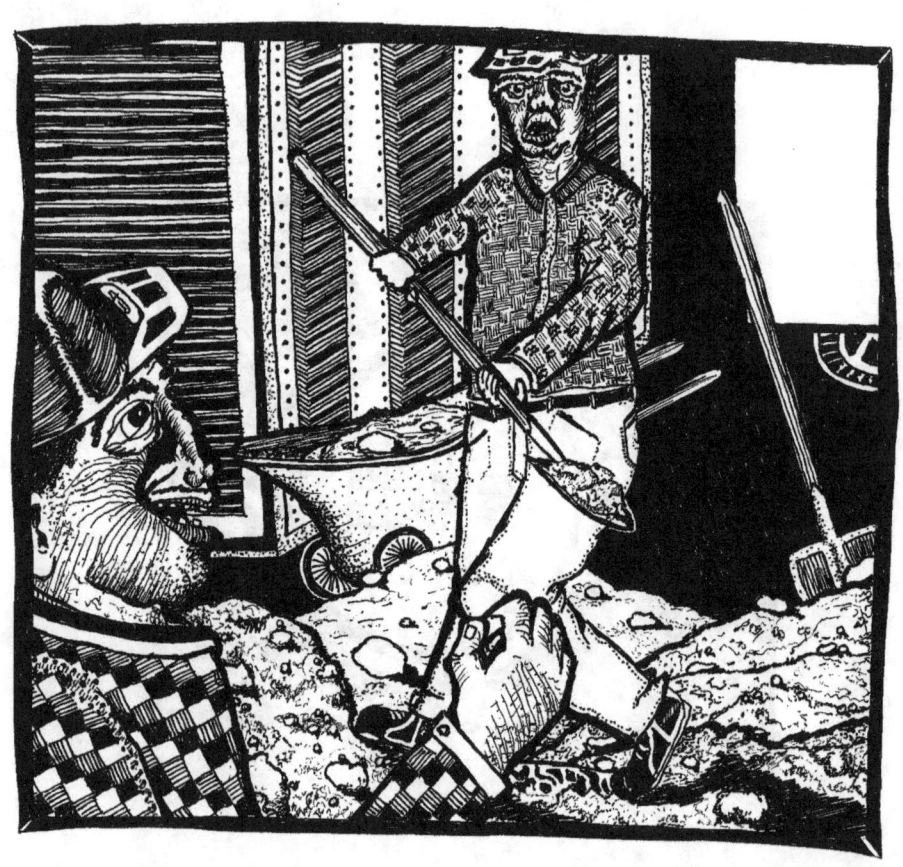

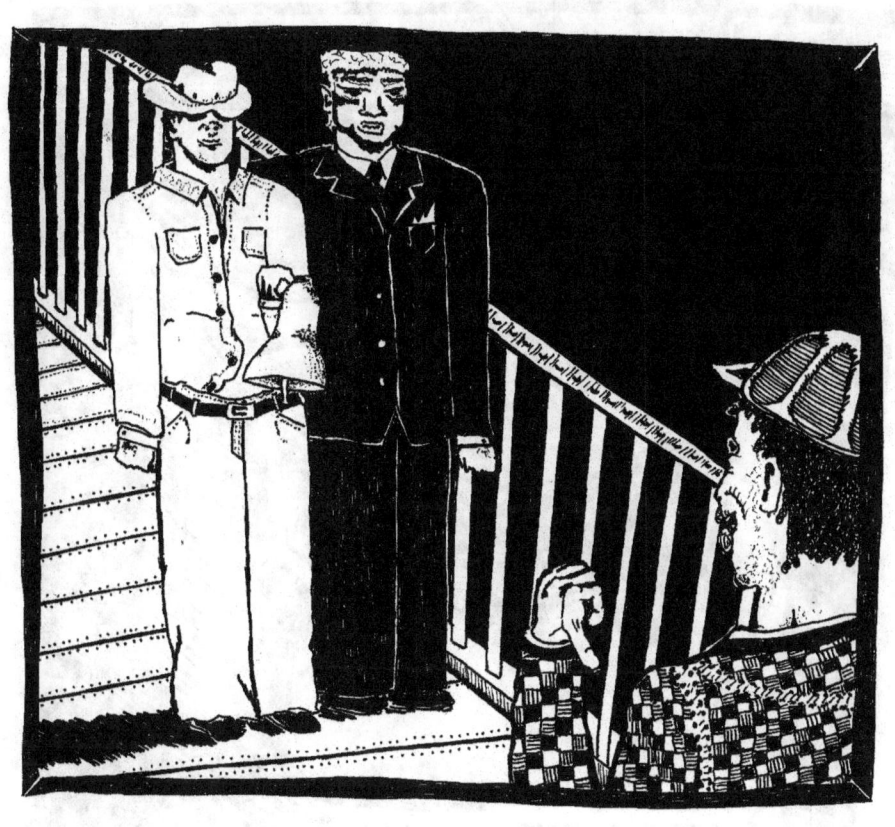

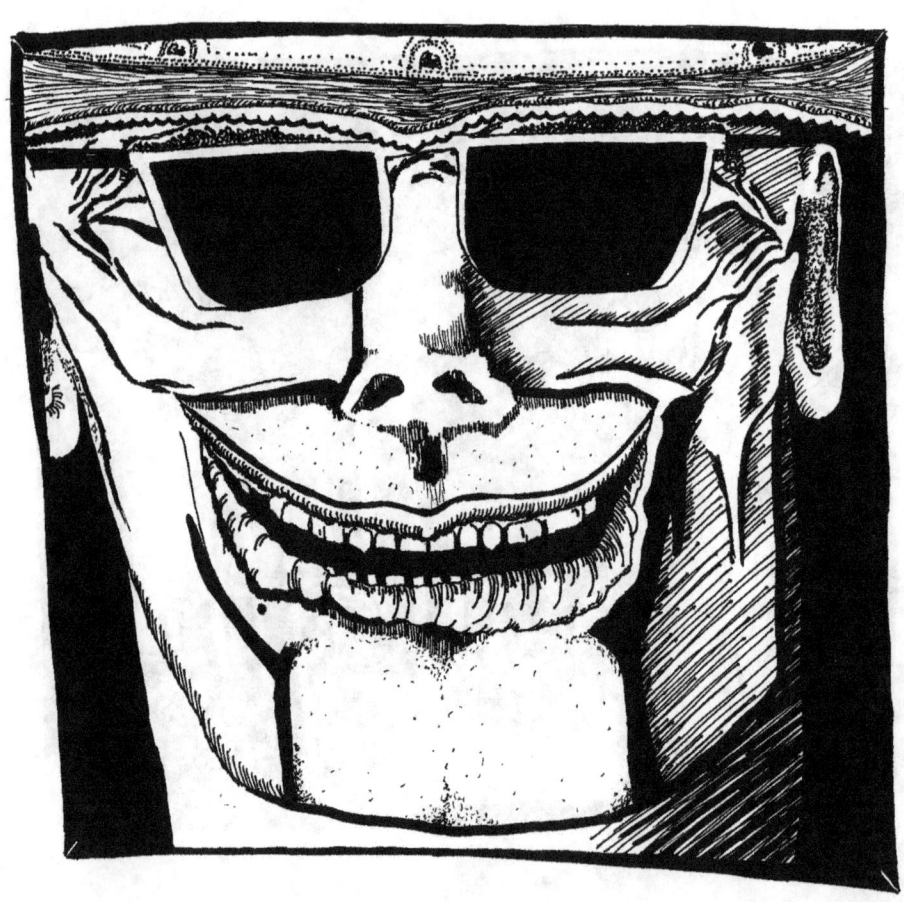

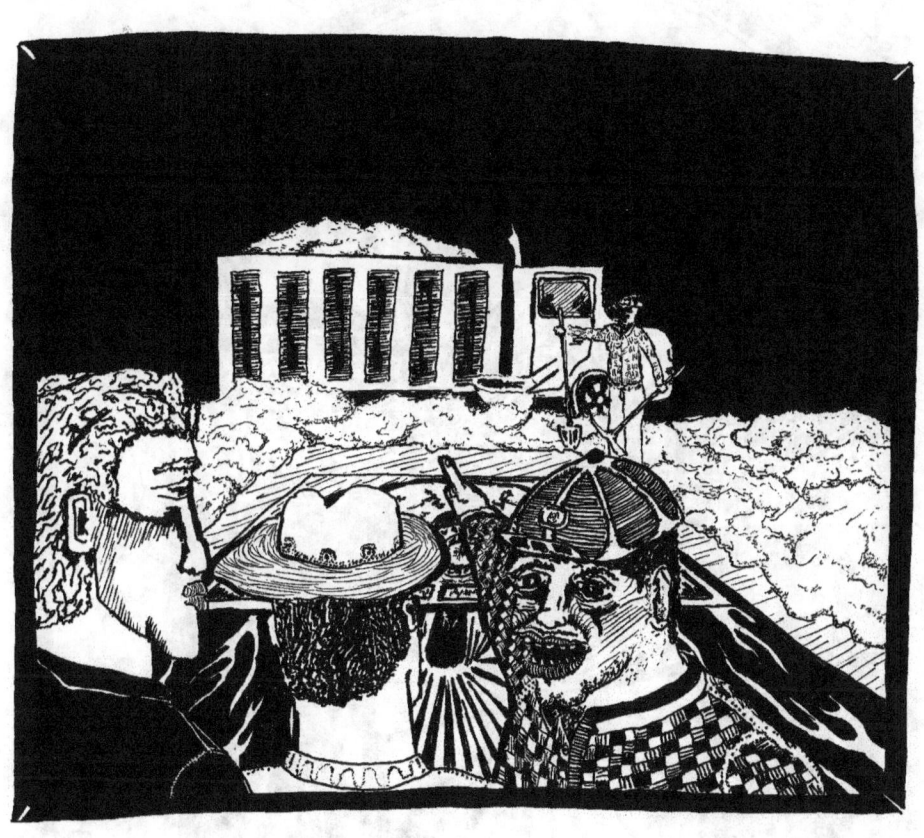

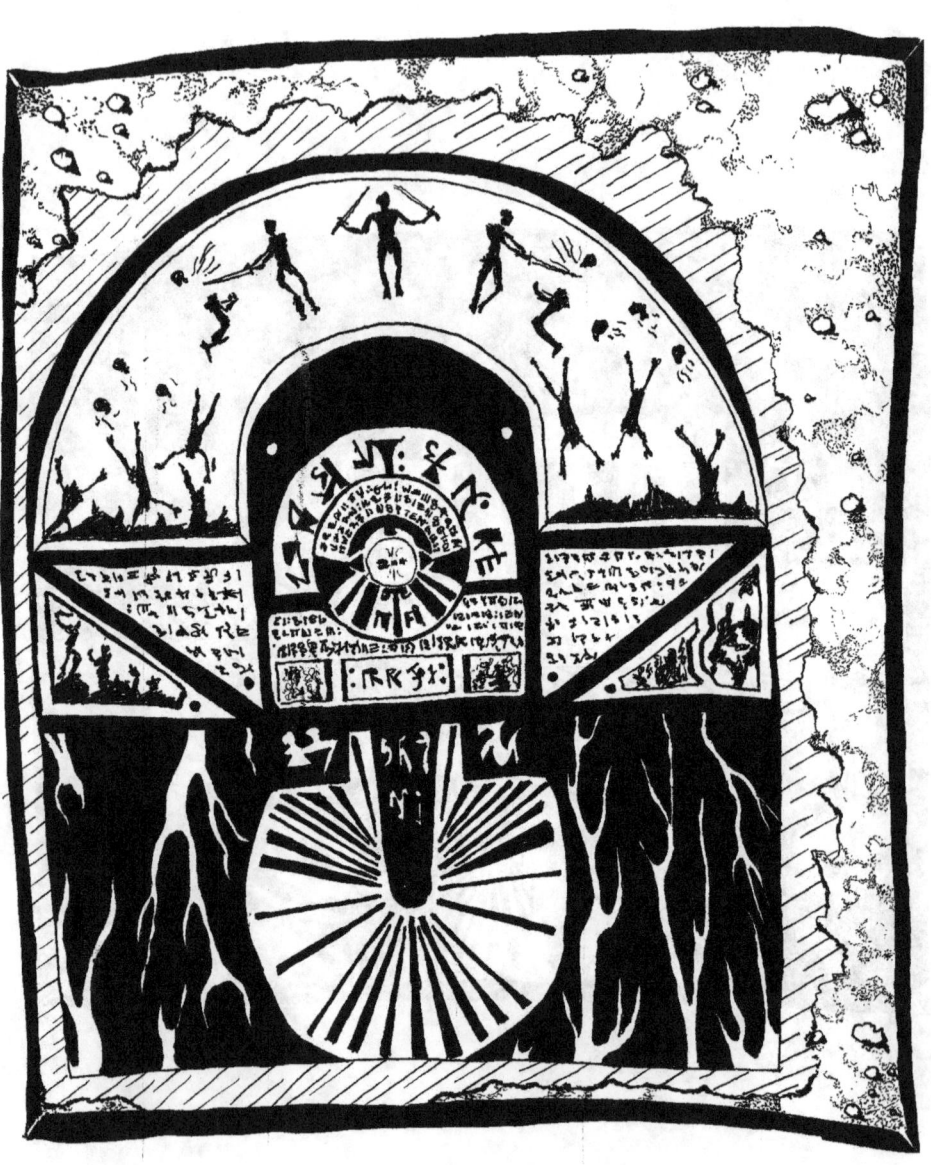

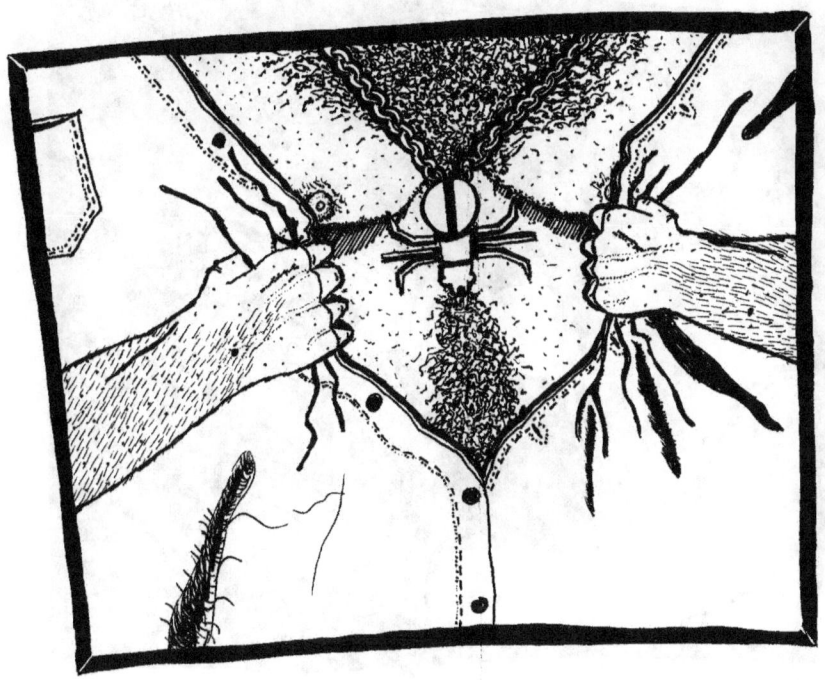

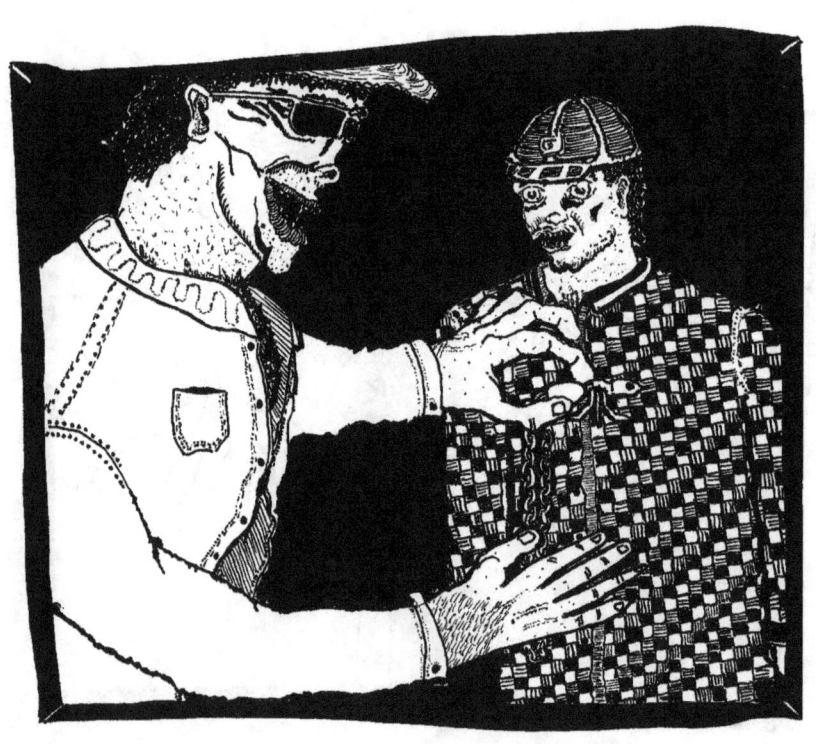

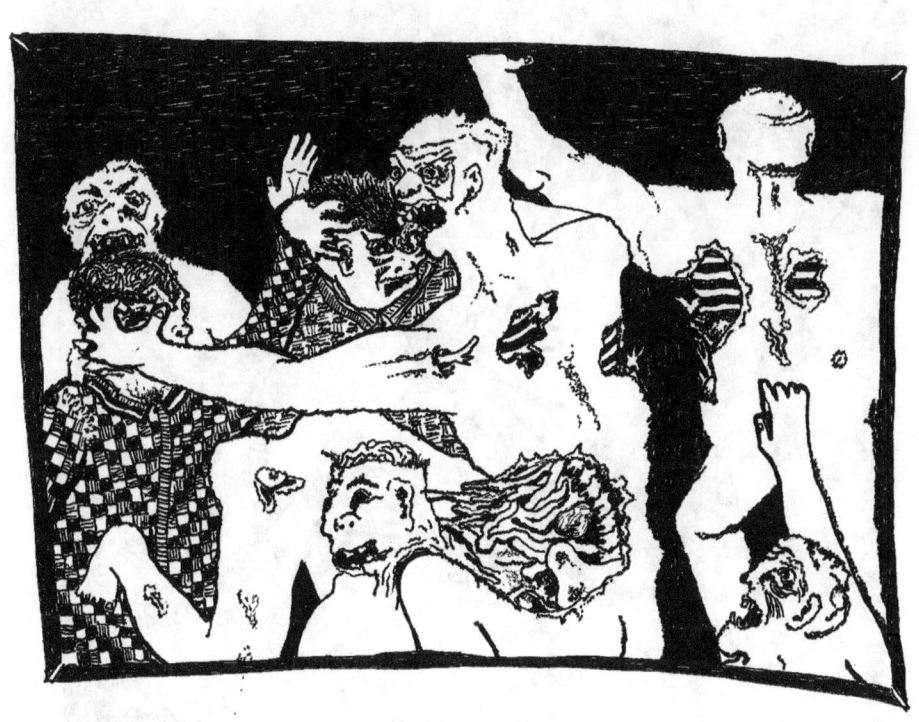

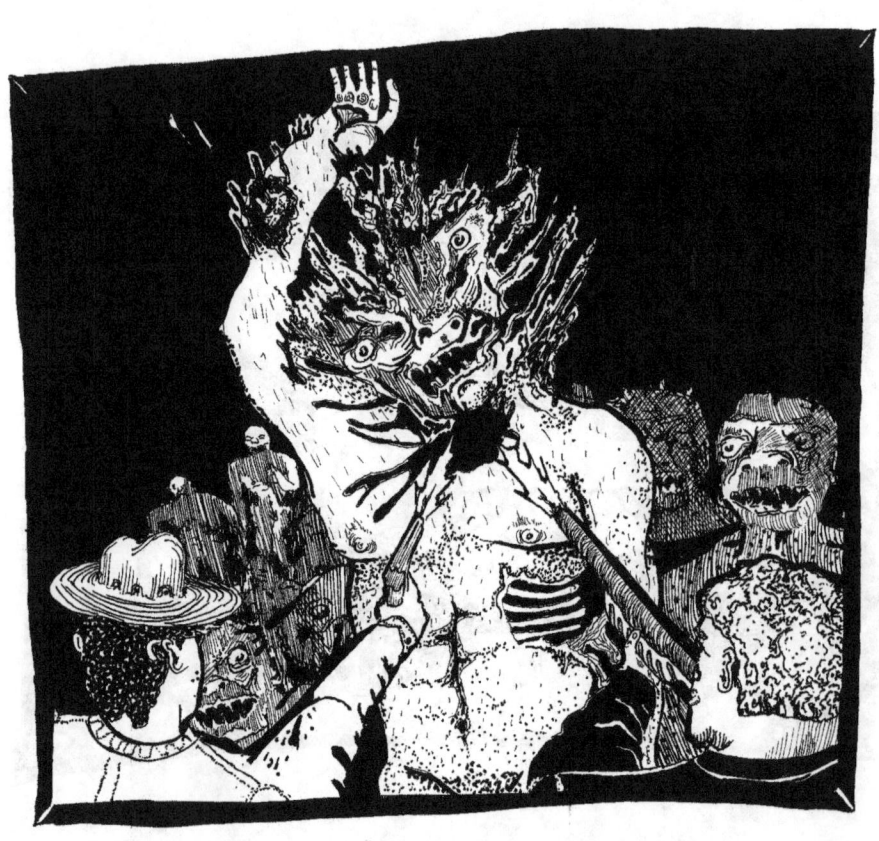

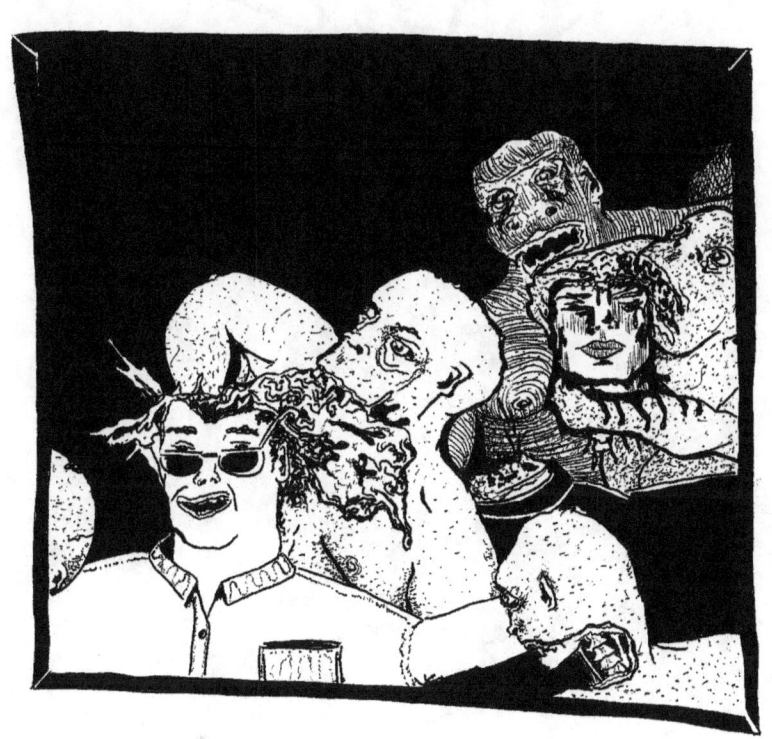

Portfolio 3

War

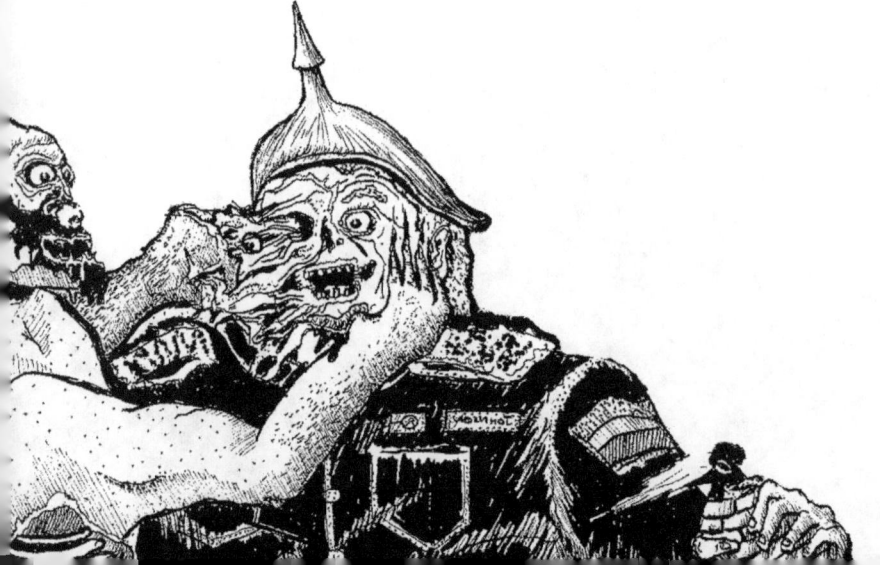

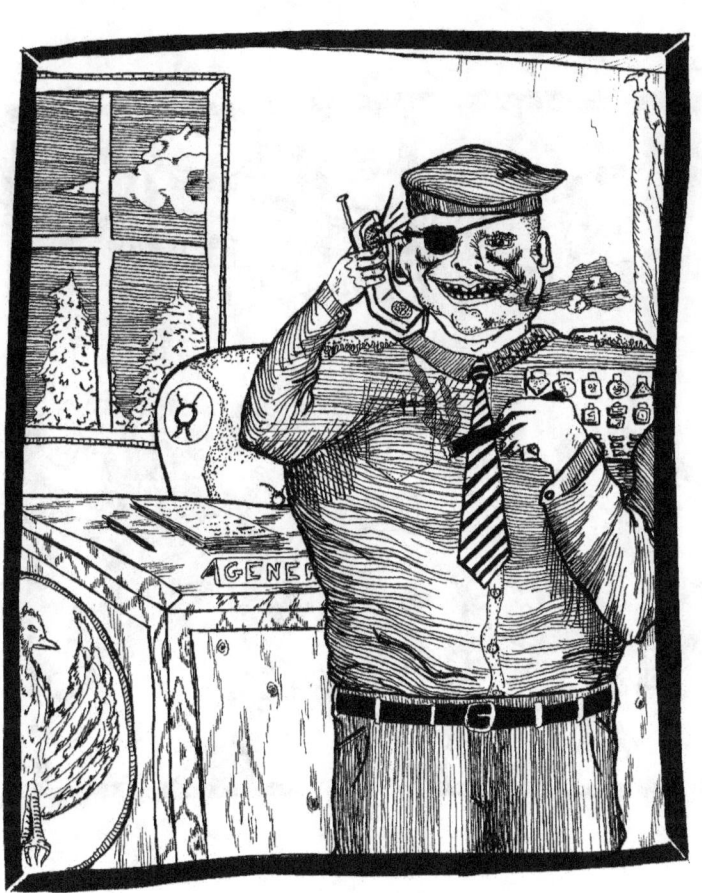

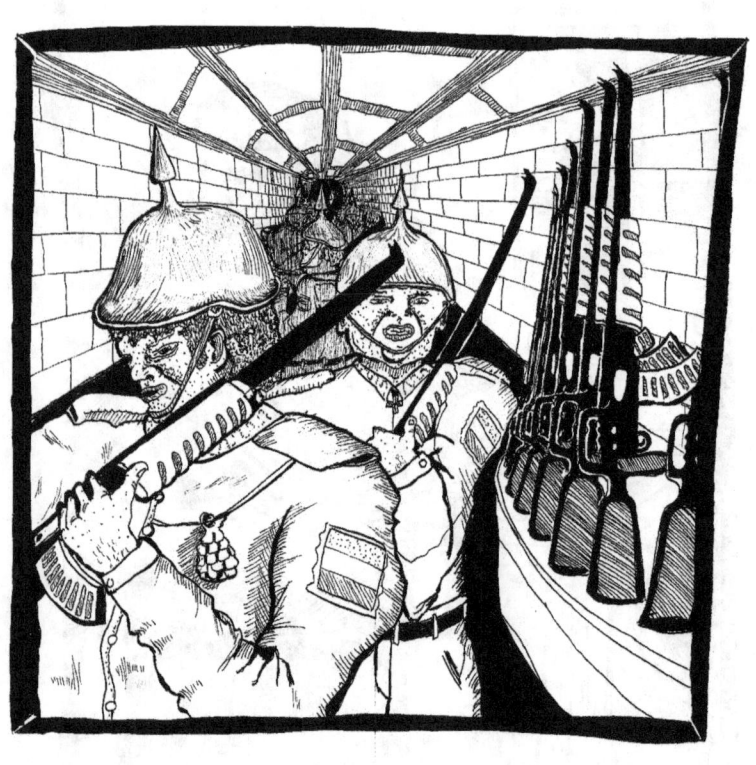

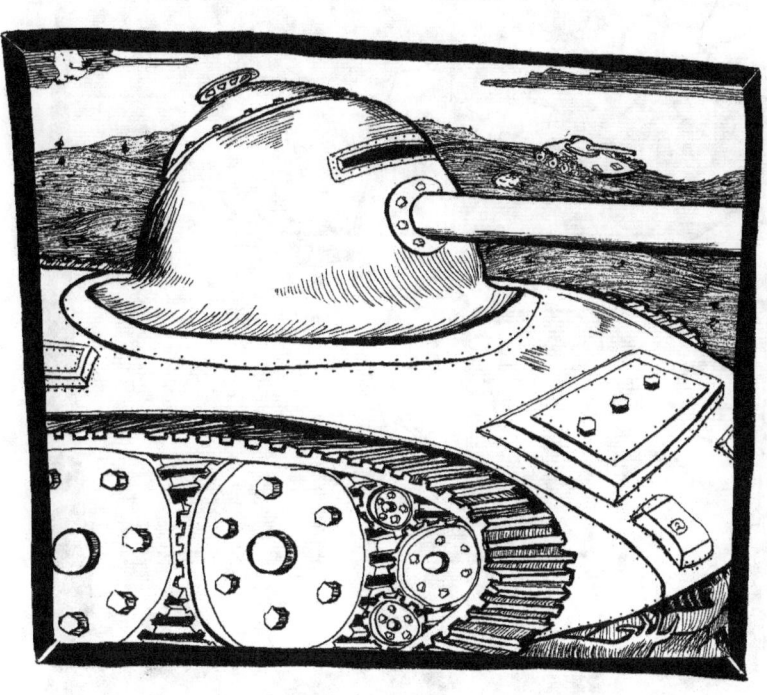

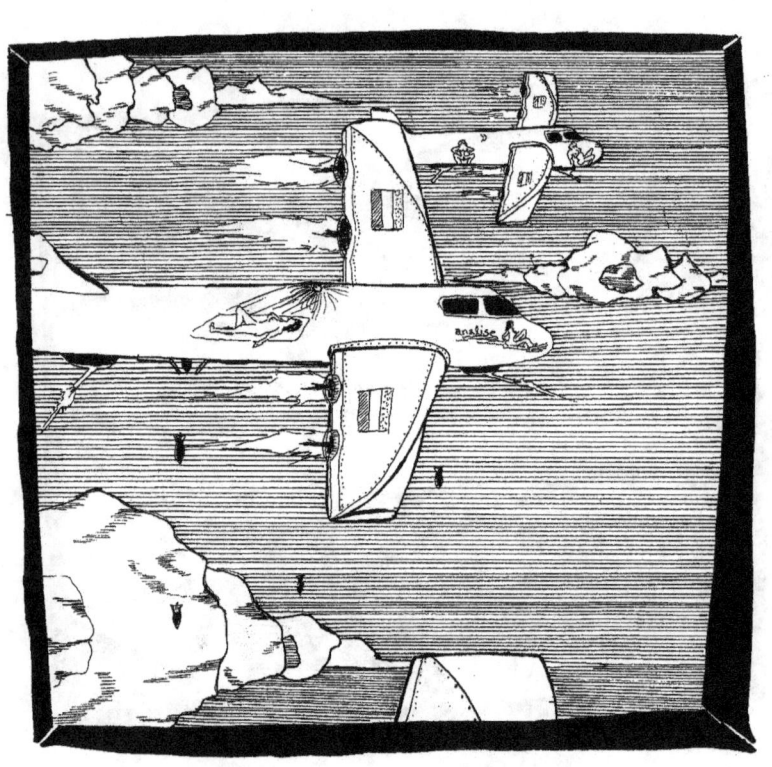

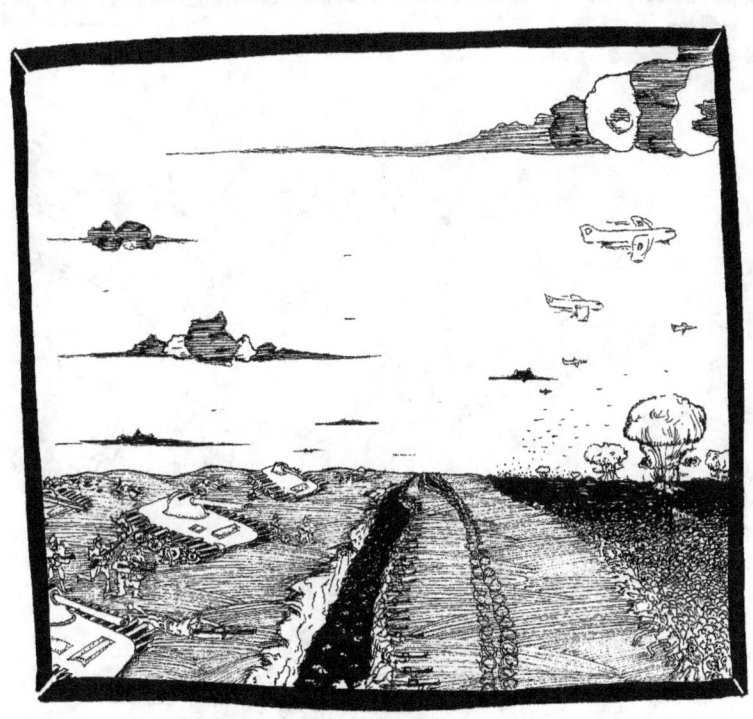

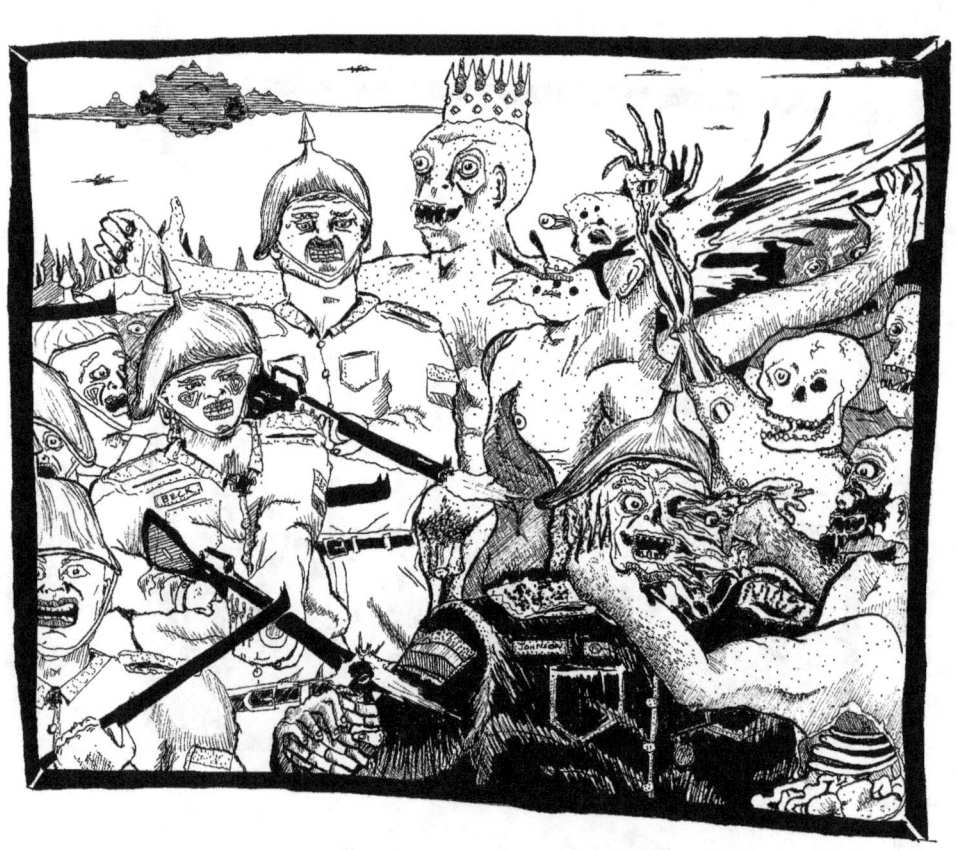

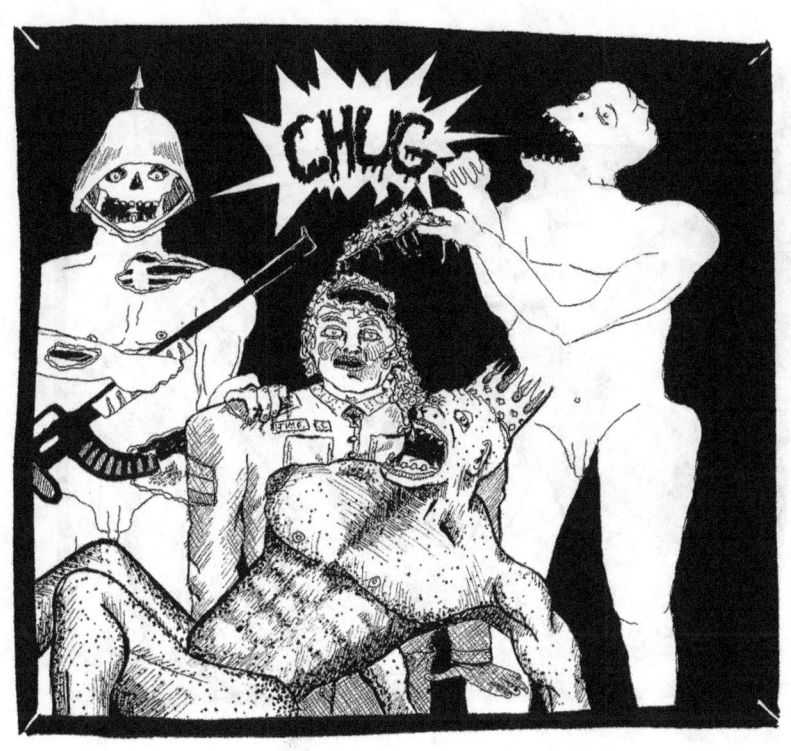

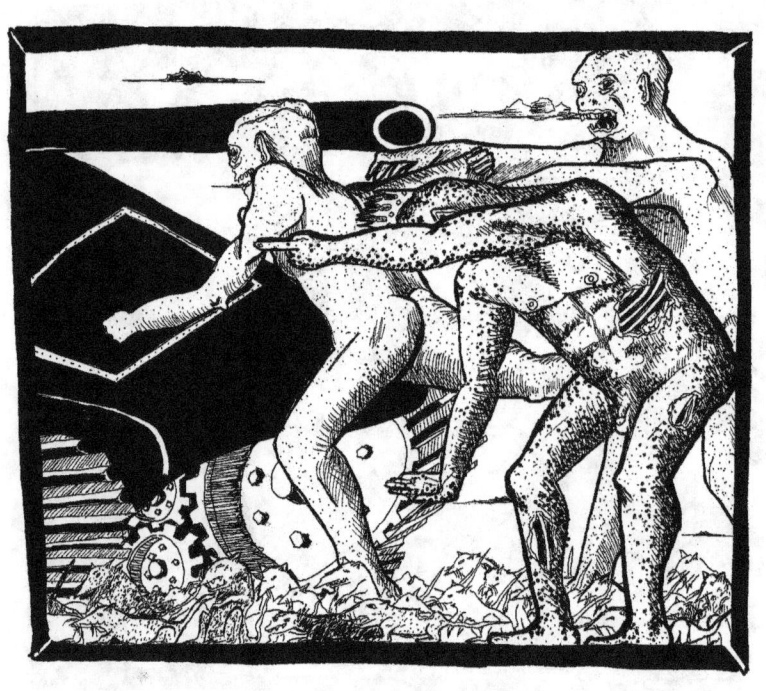

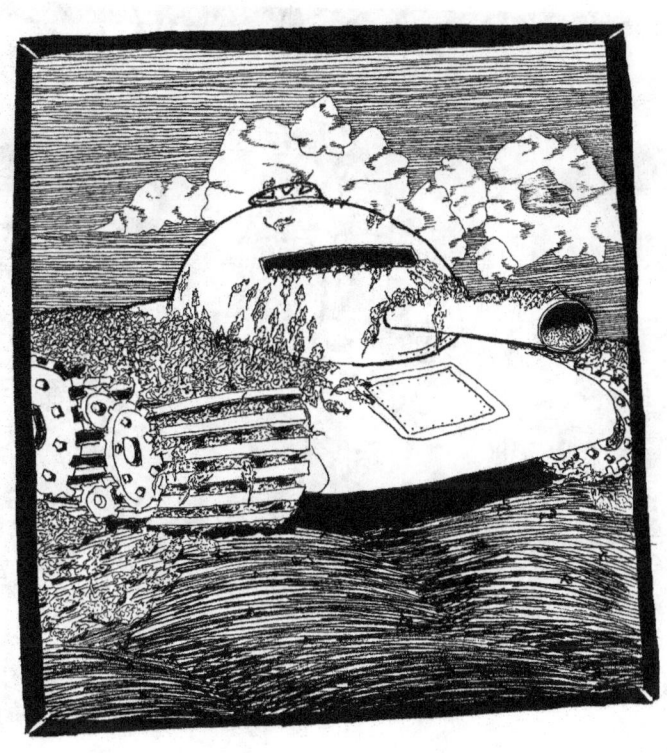

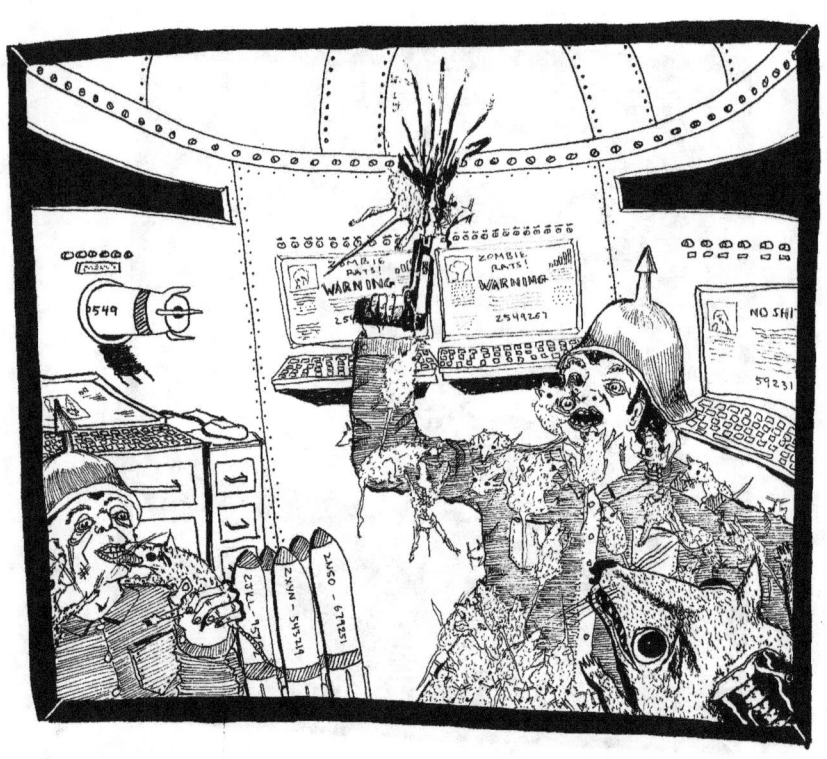

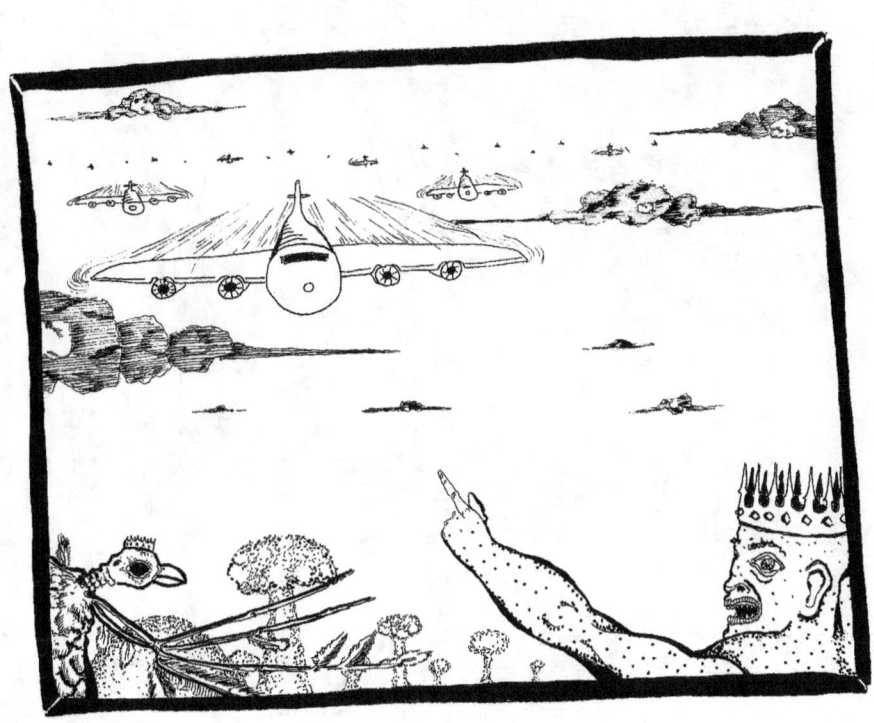

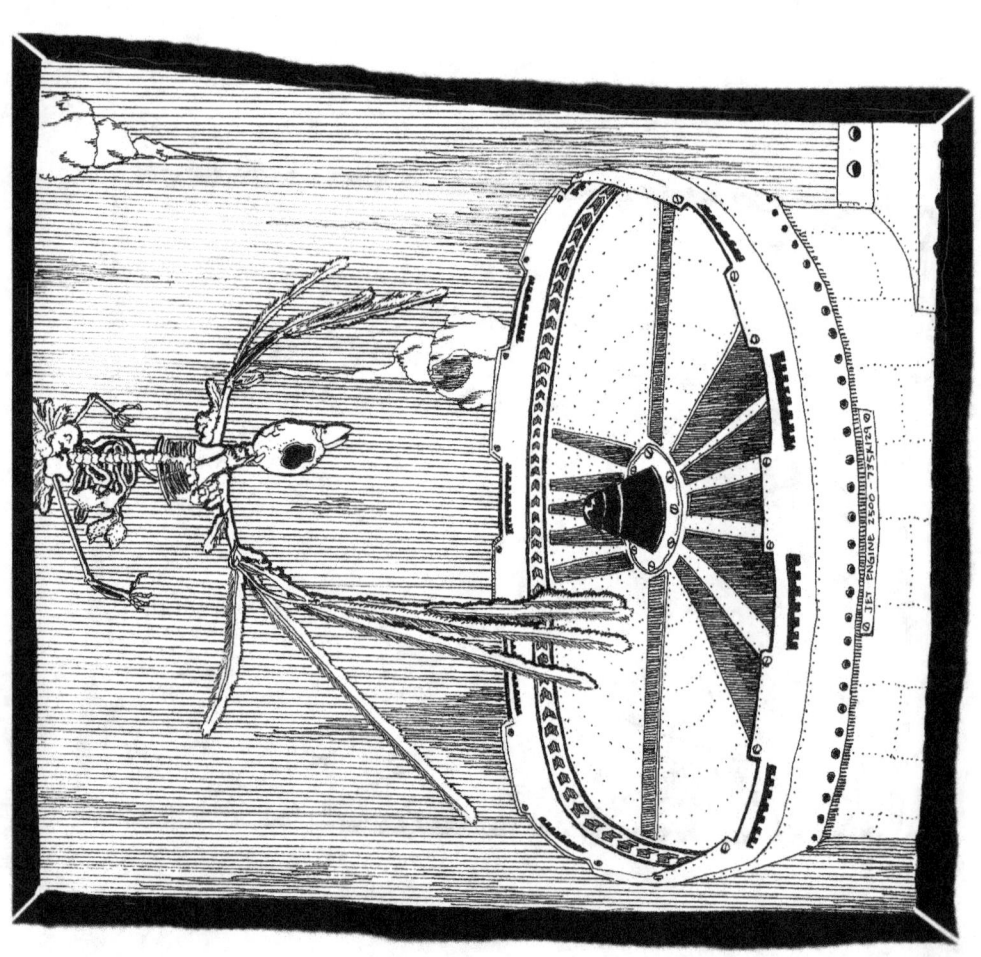

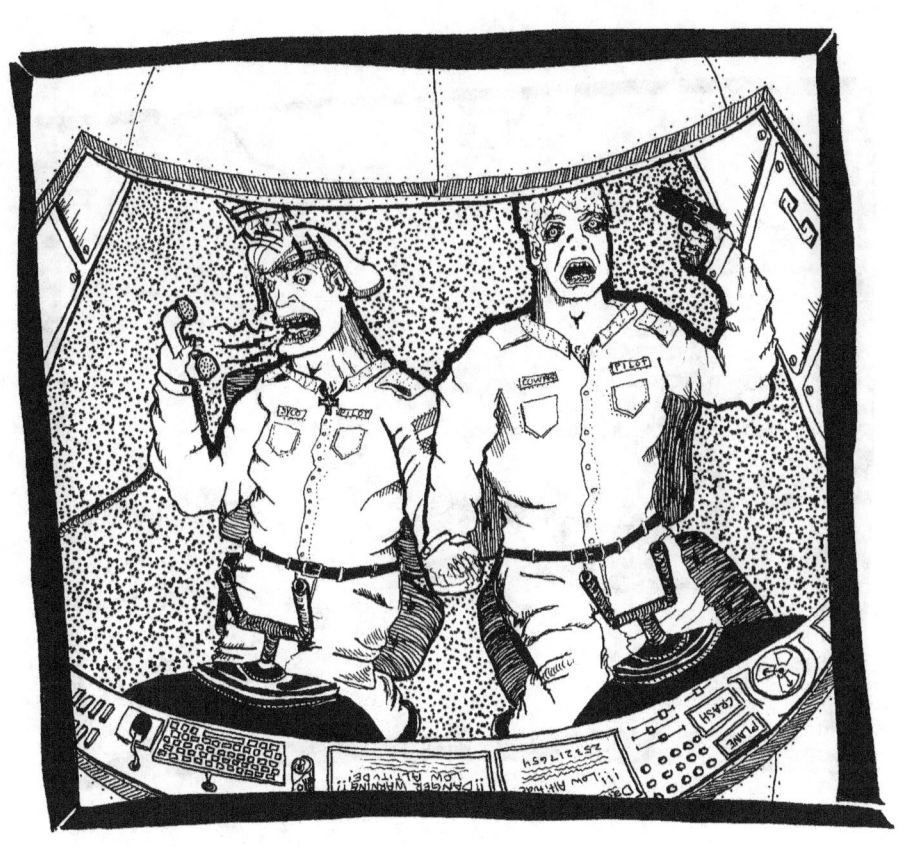

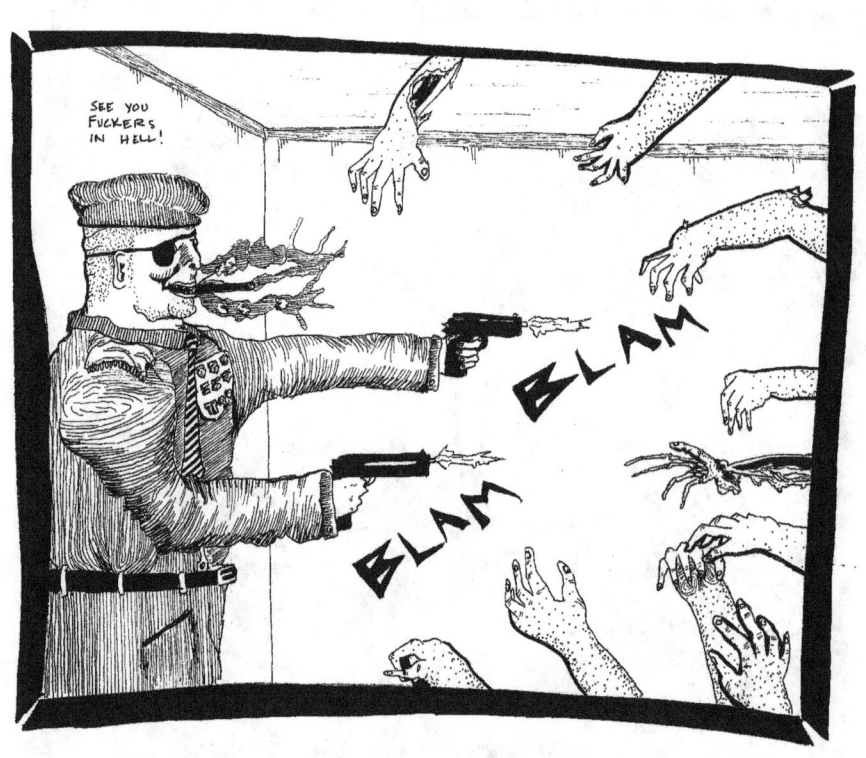

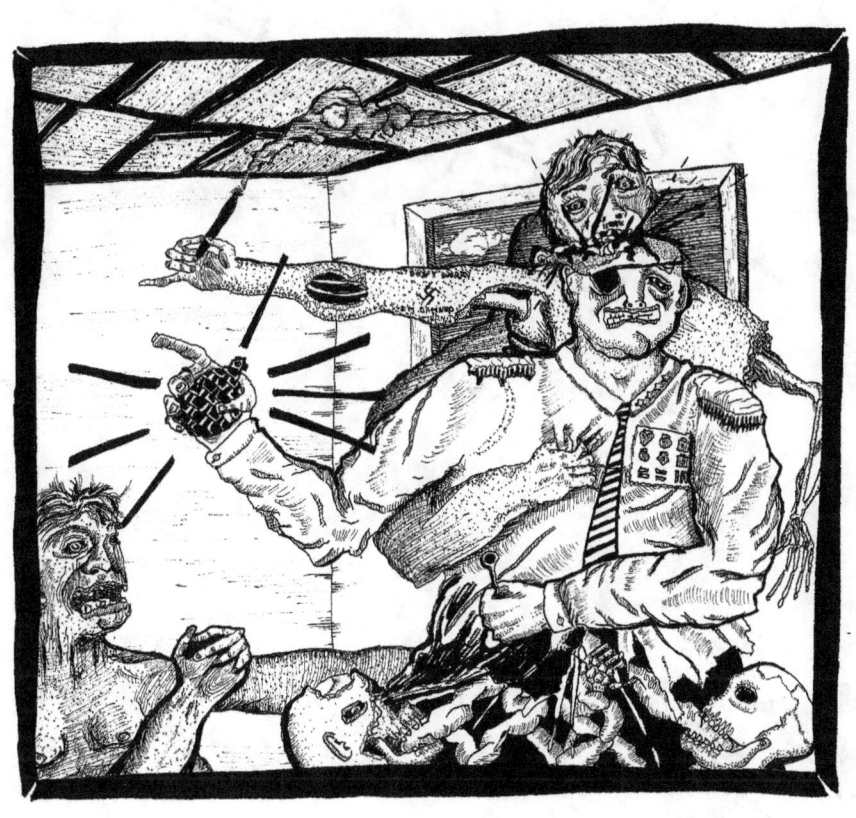

Portfolio A

Science

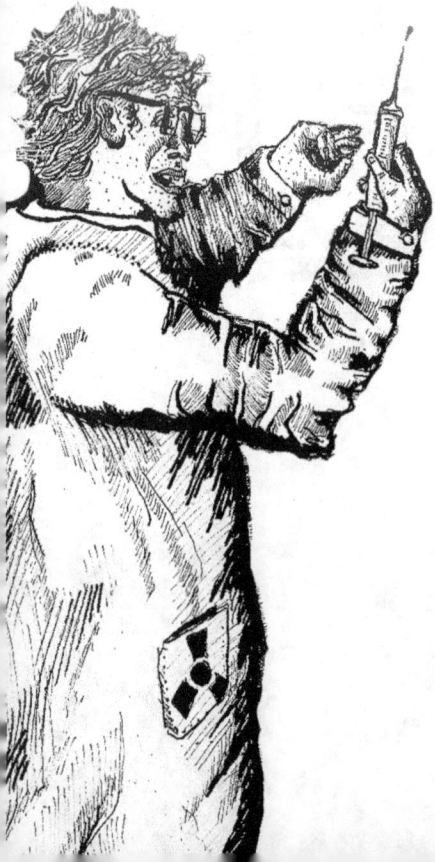

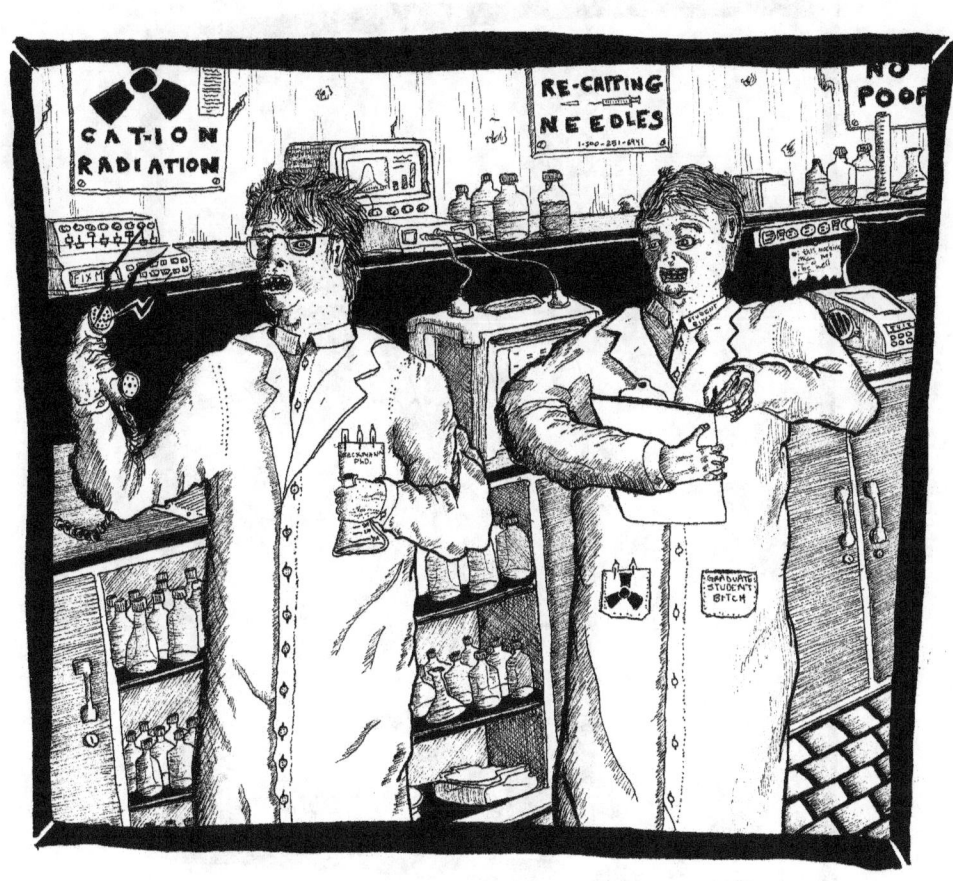

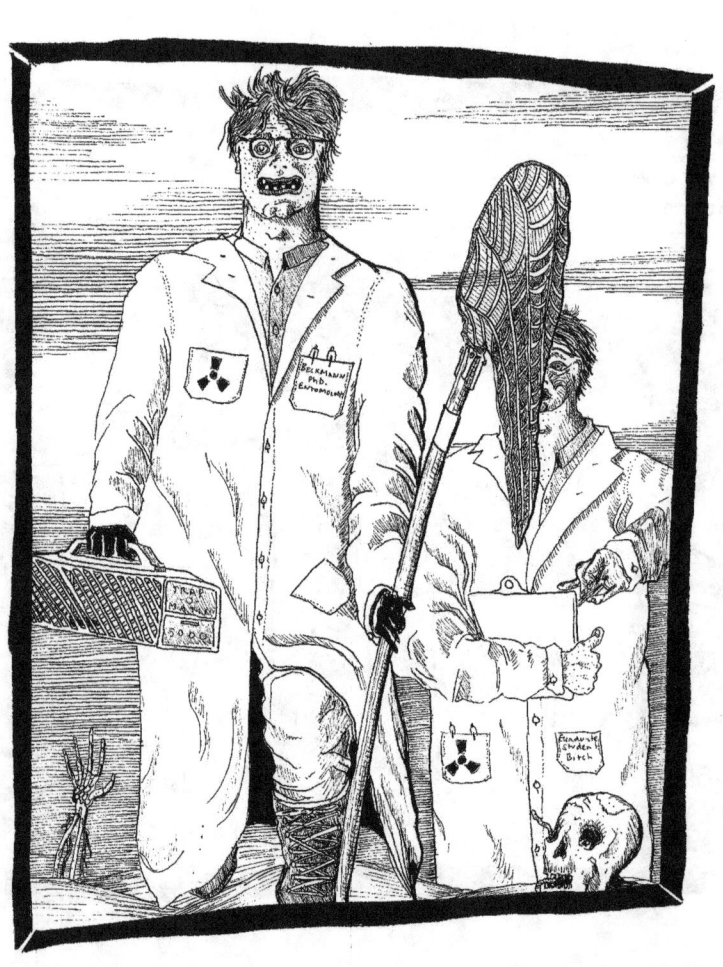

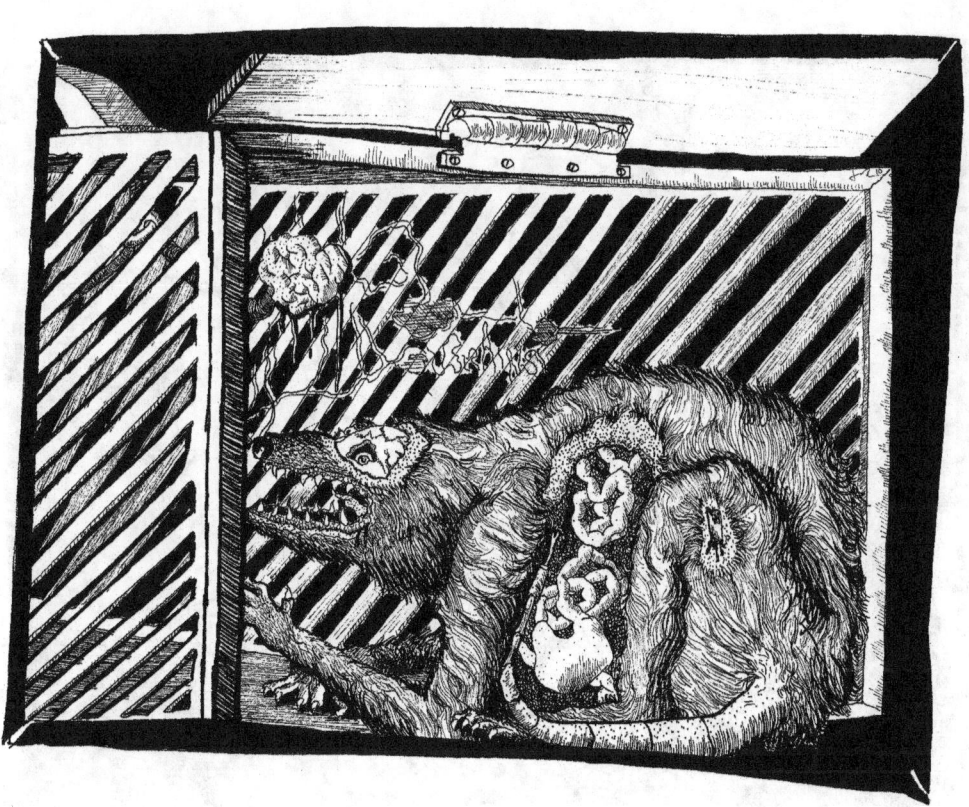

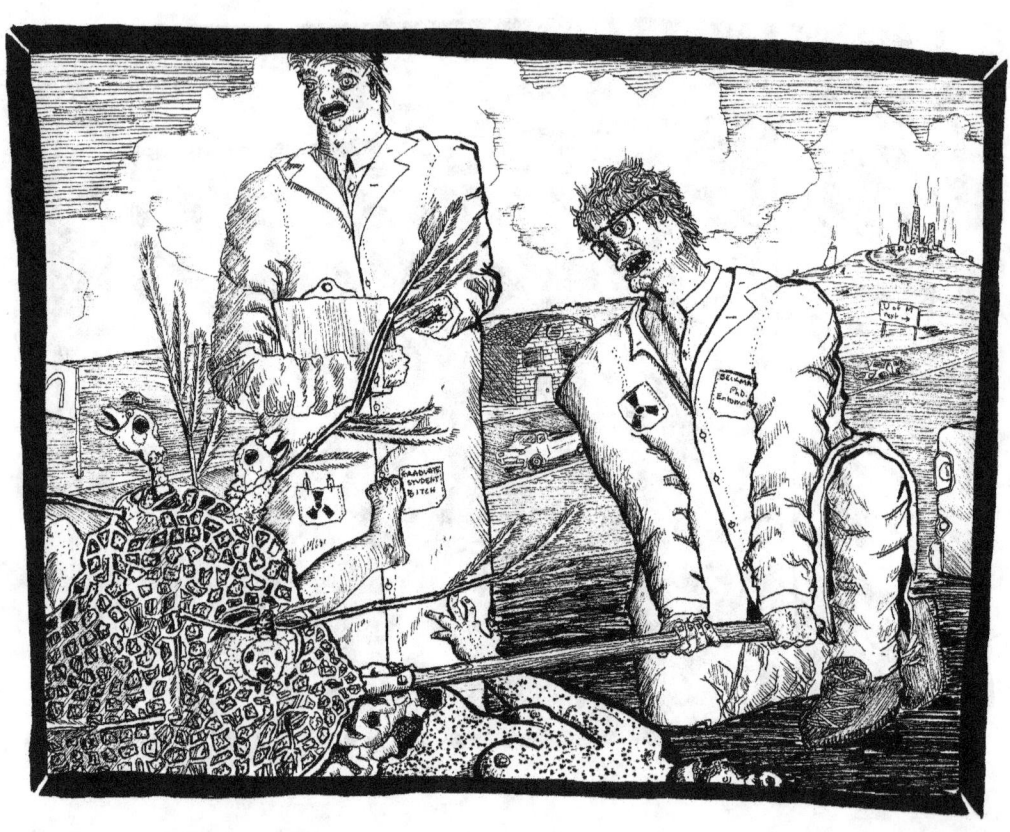

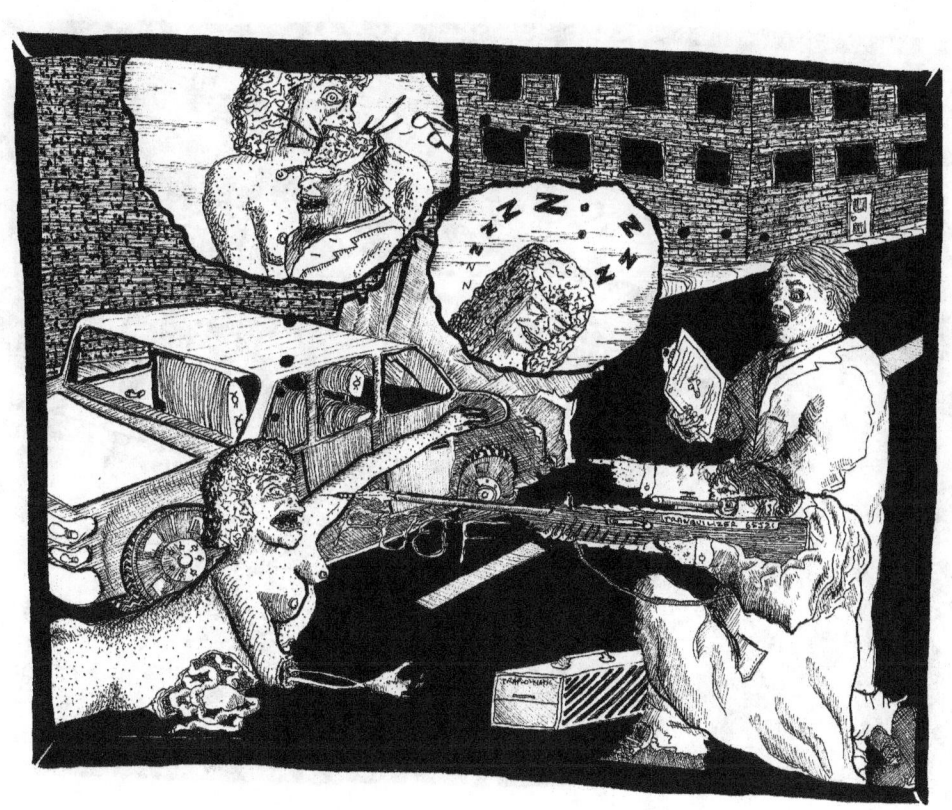

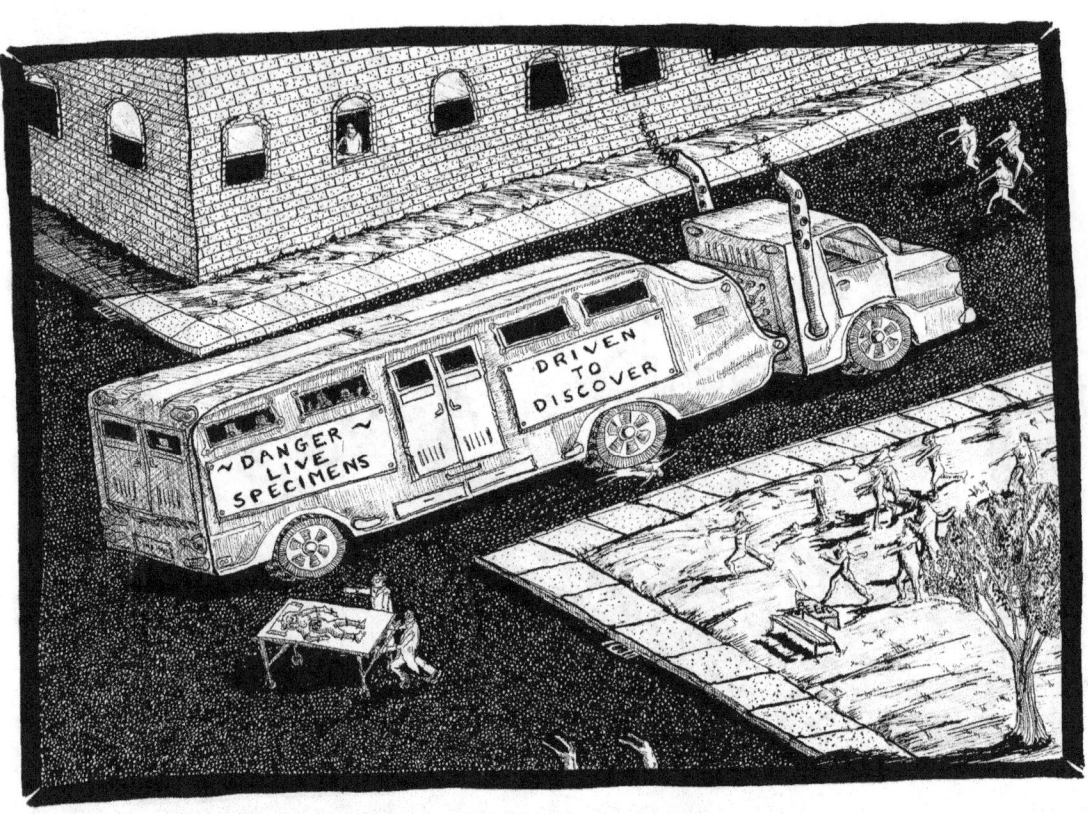

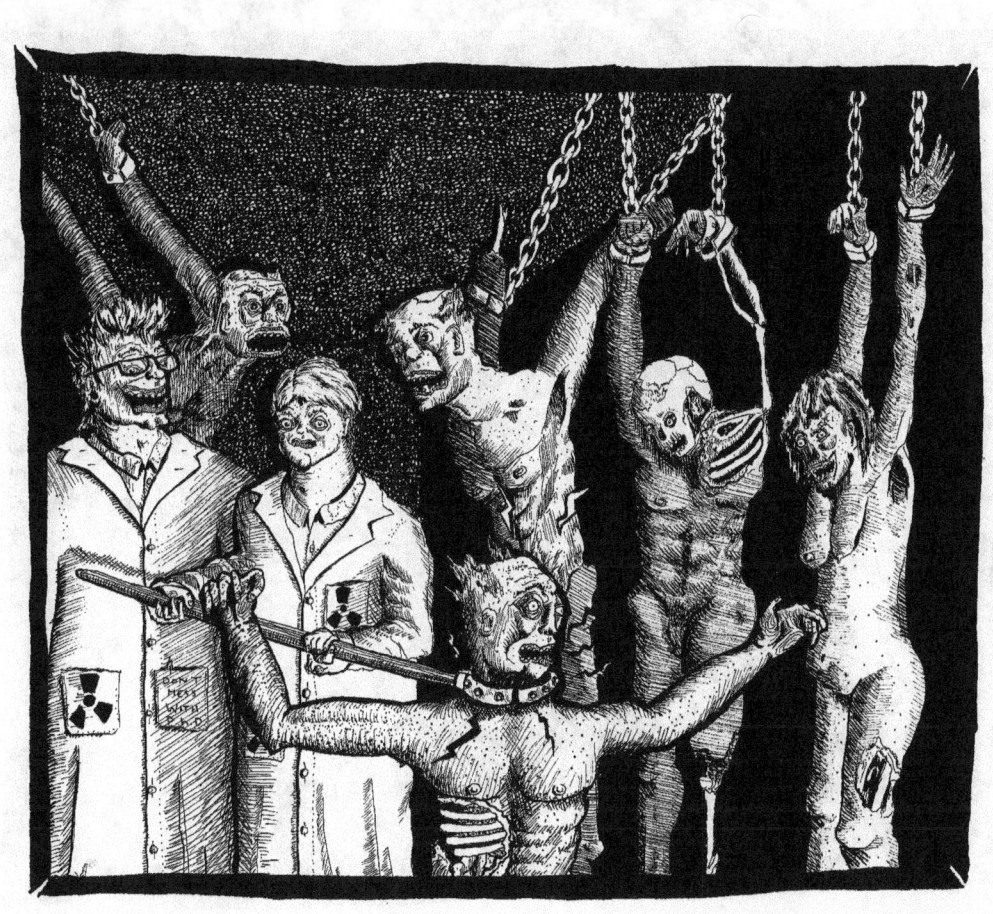

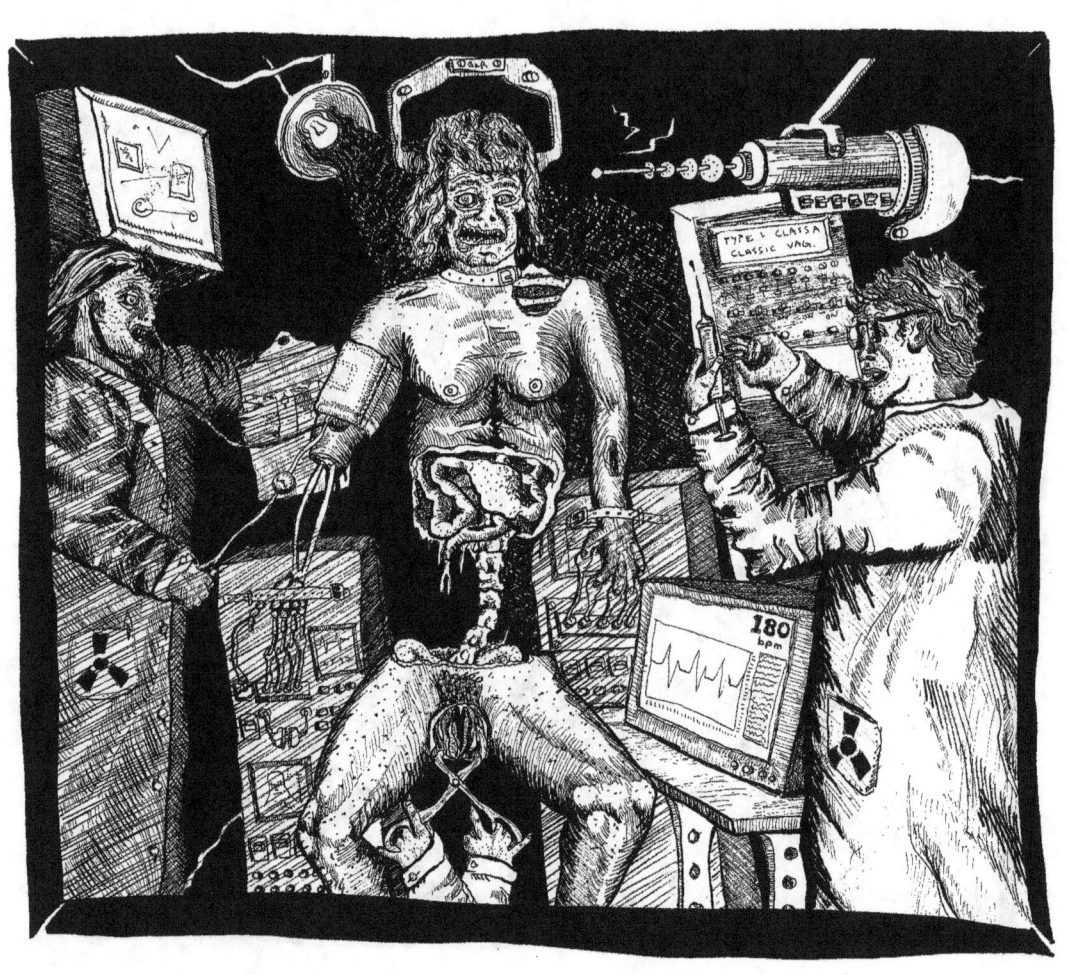

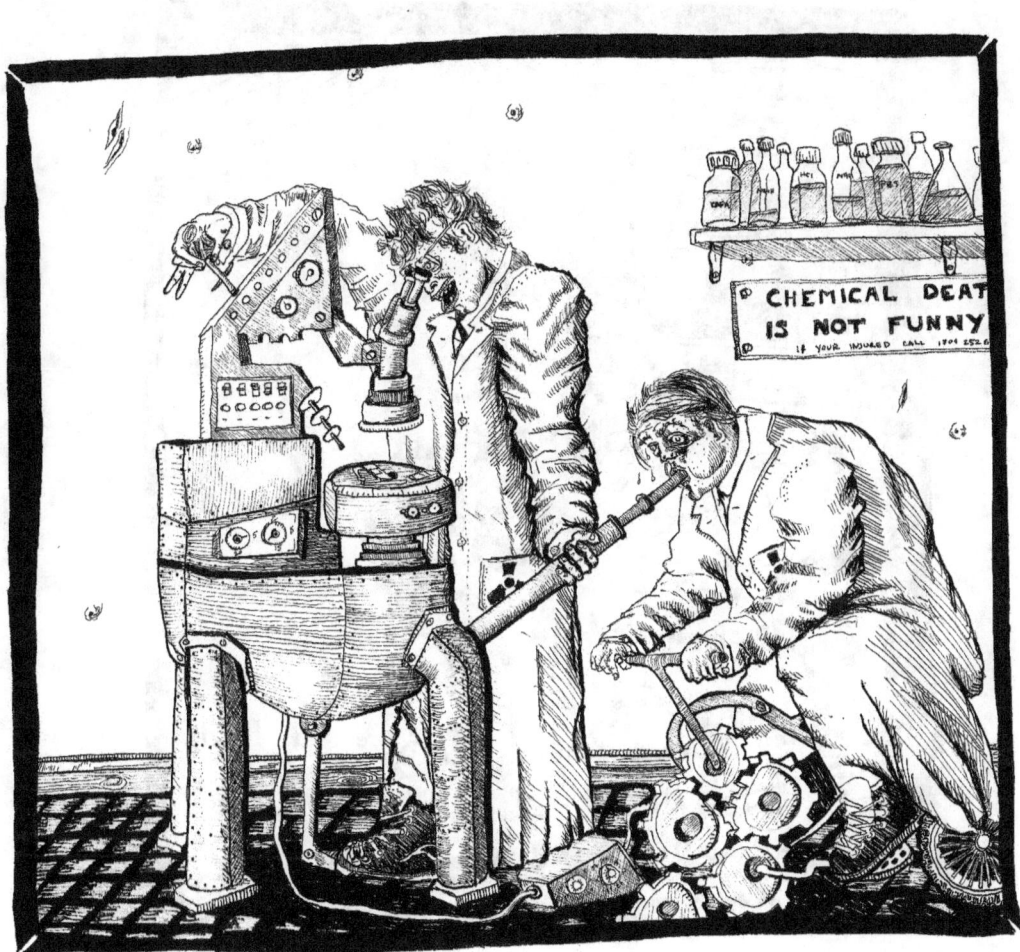

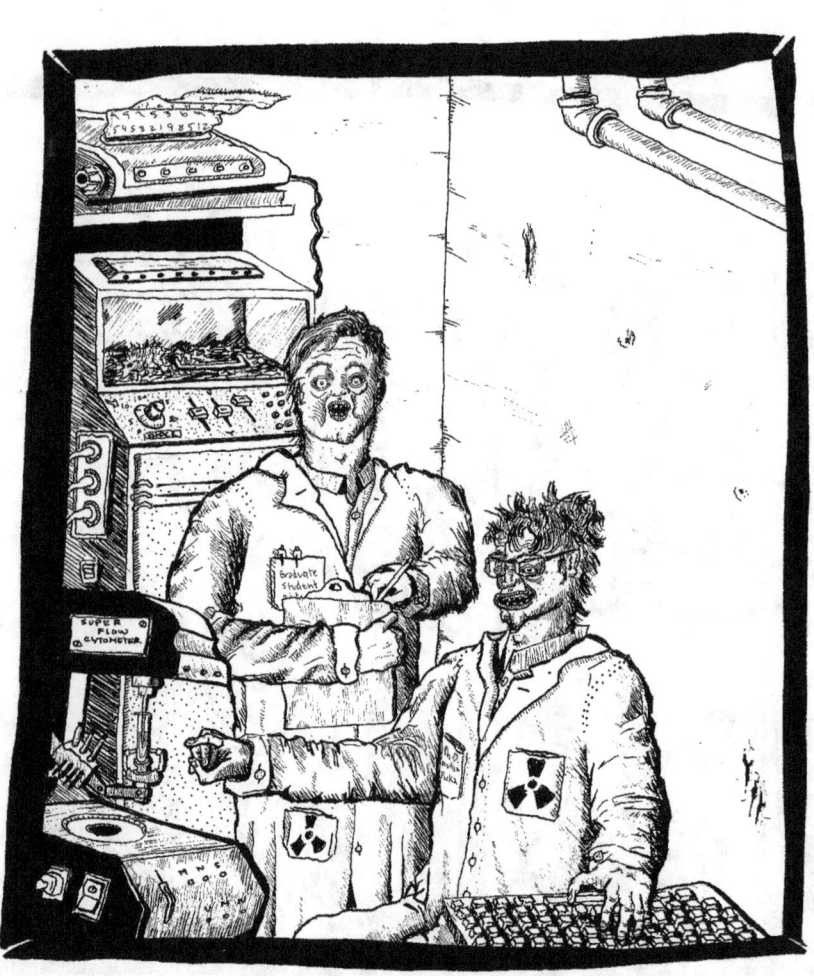

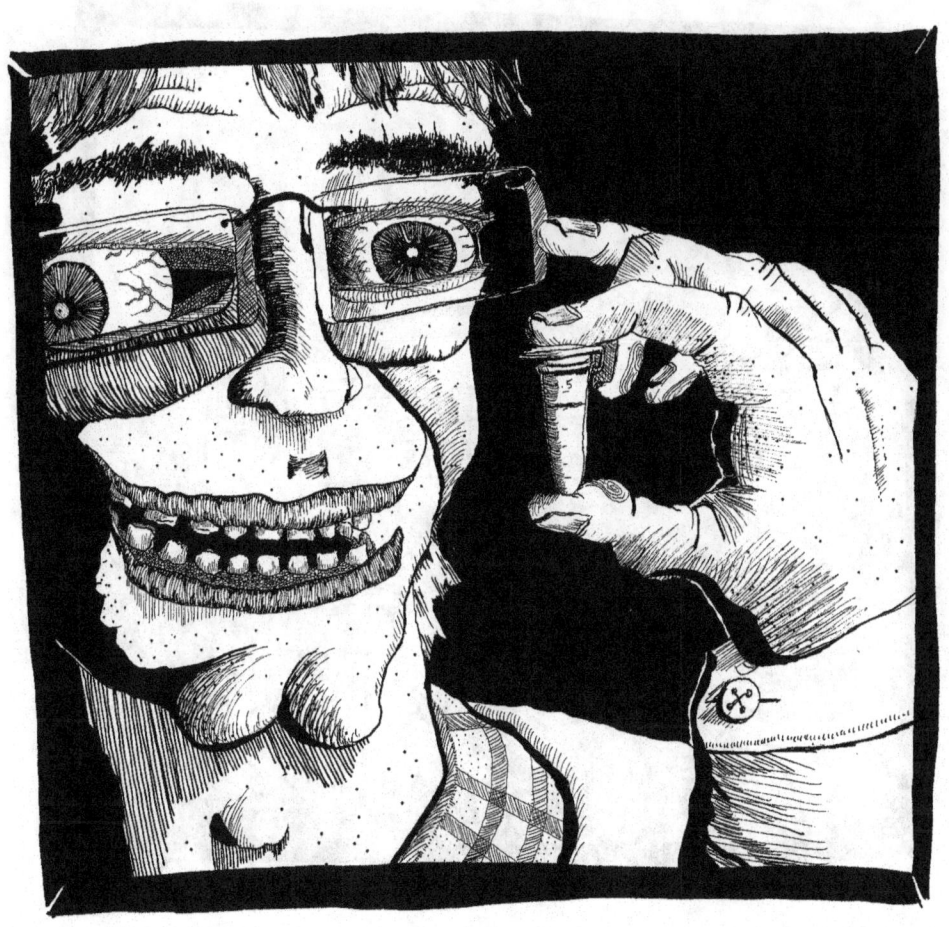

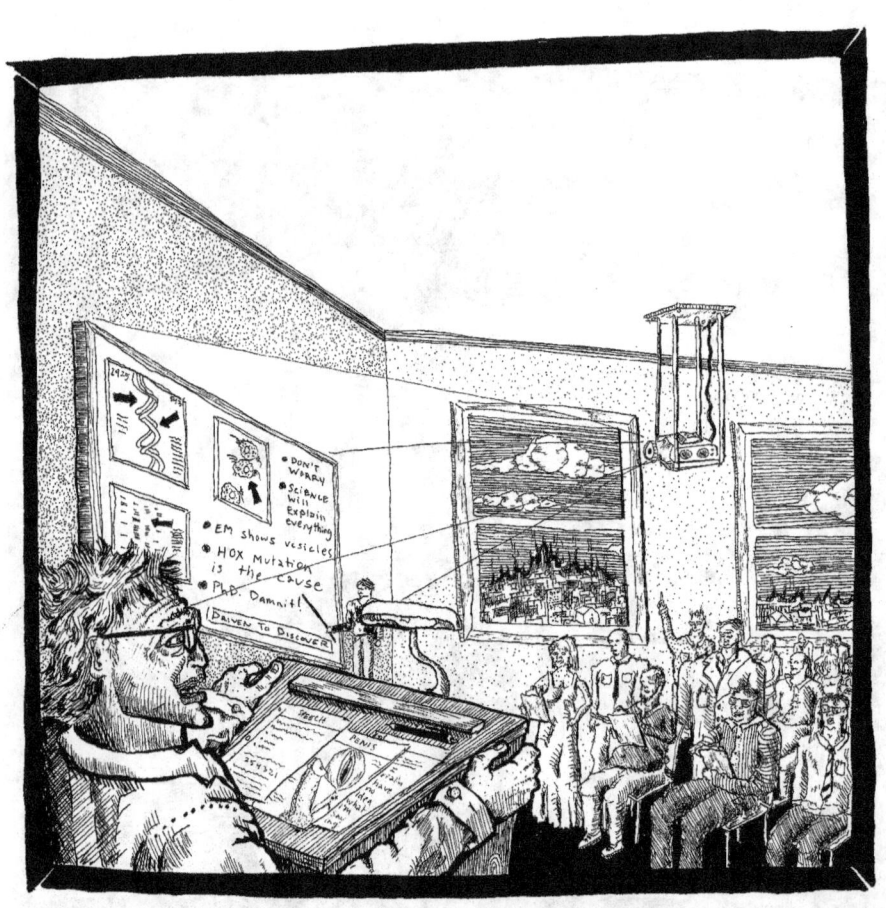

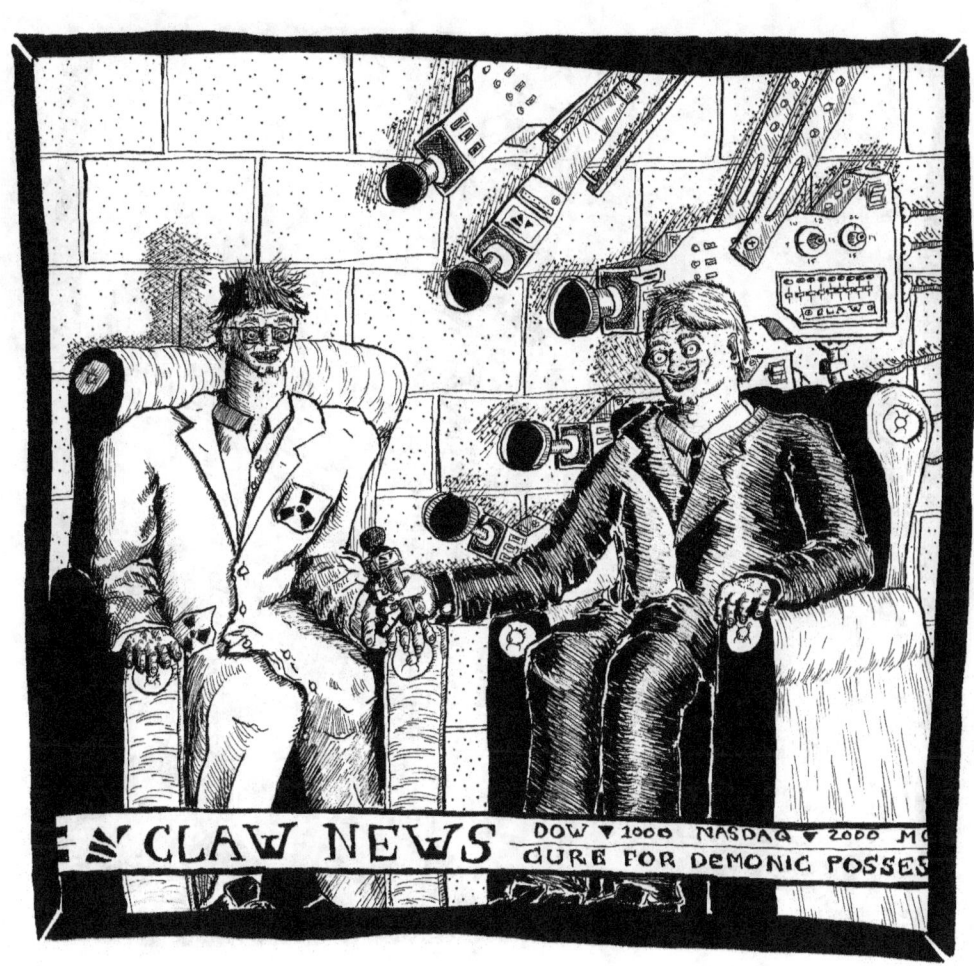

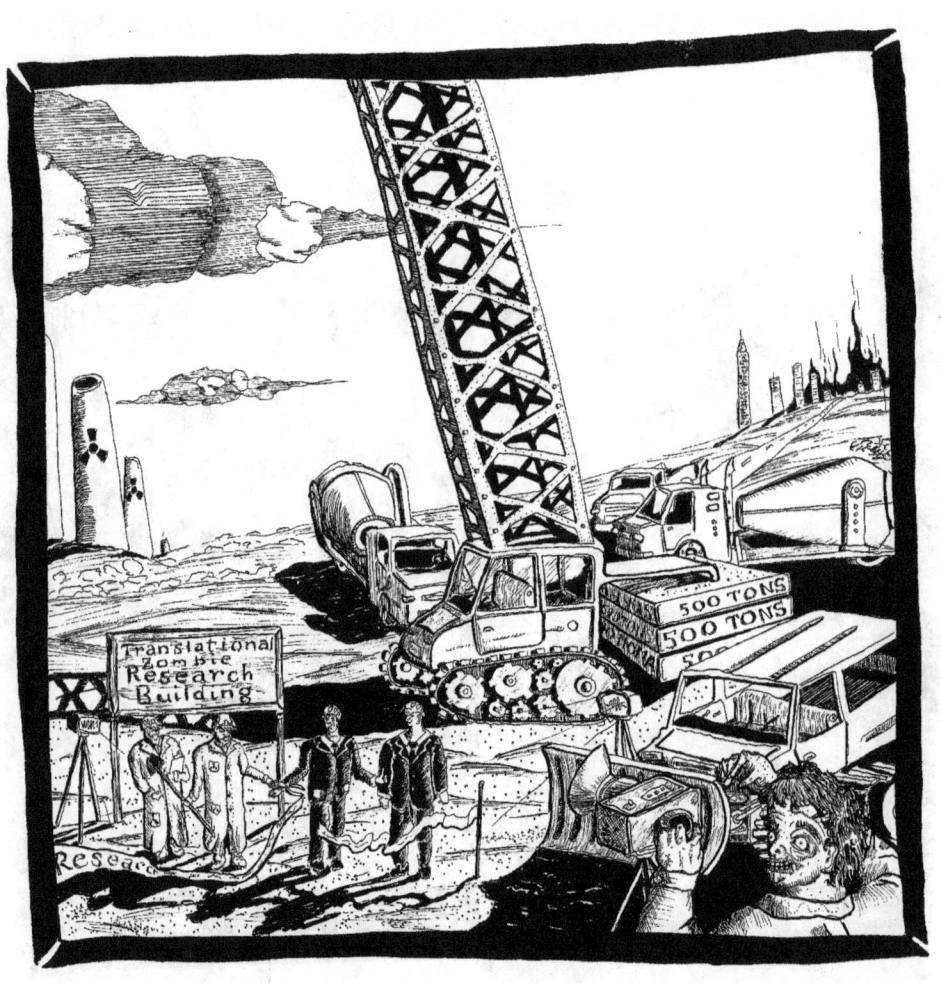

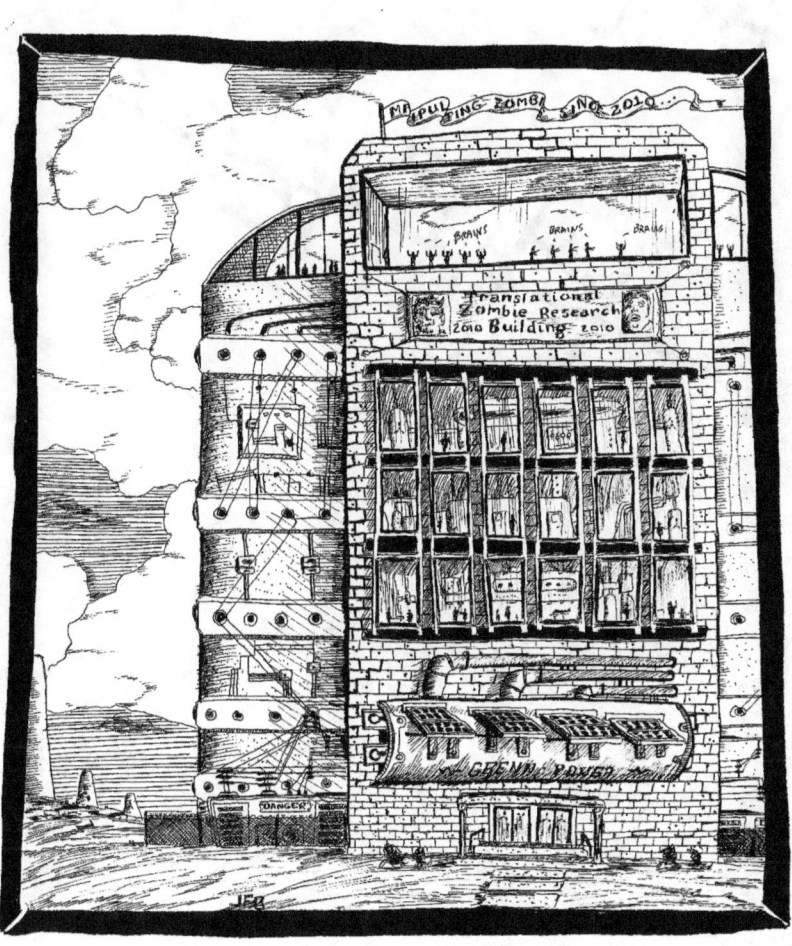

Portfolio 5

Hippies

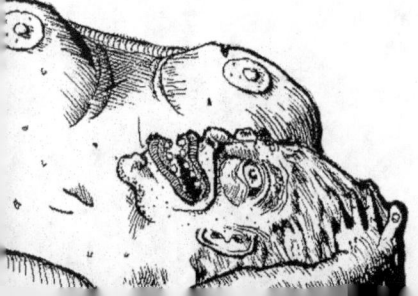

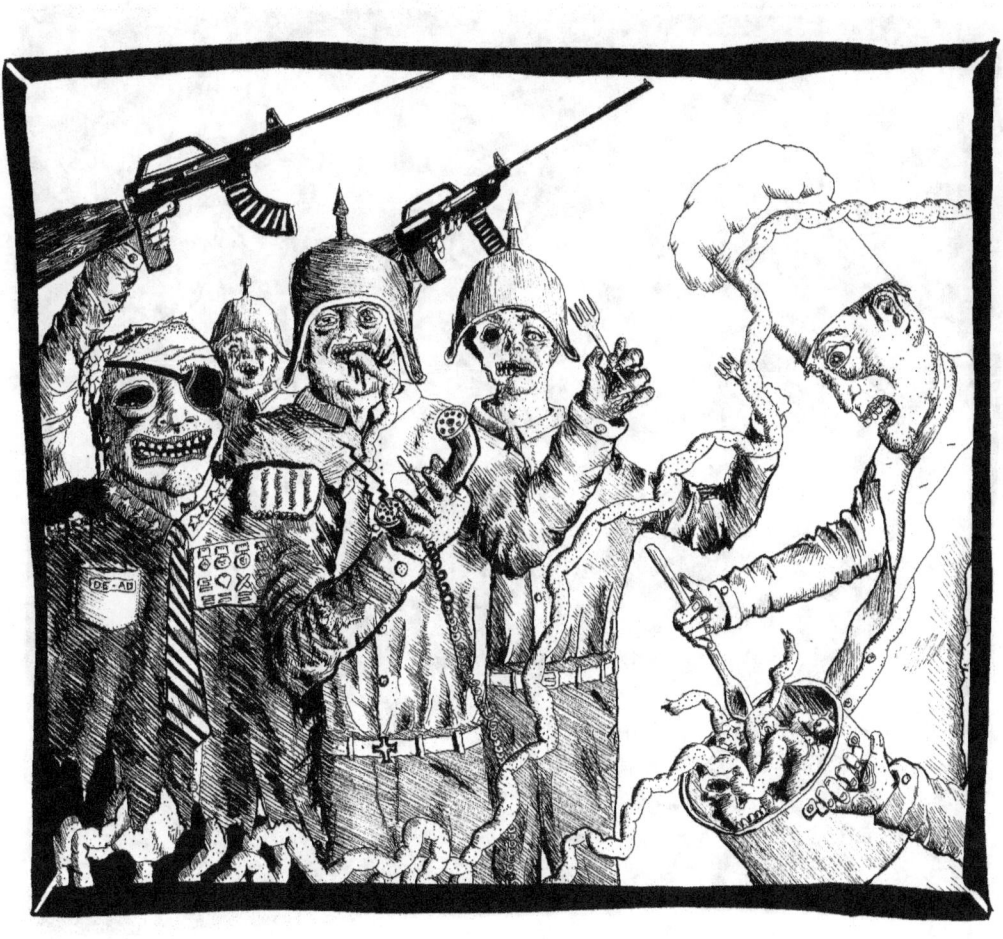

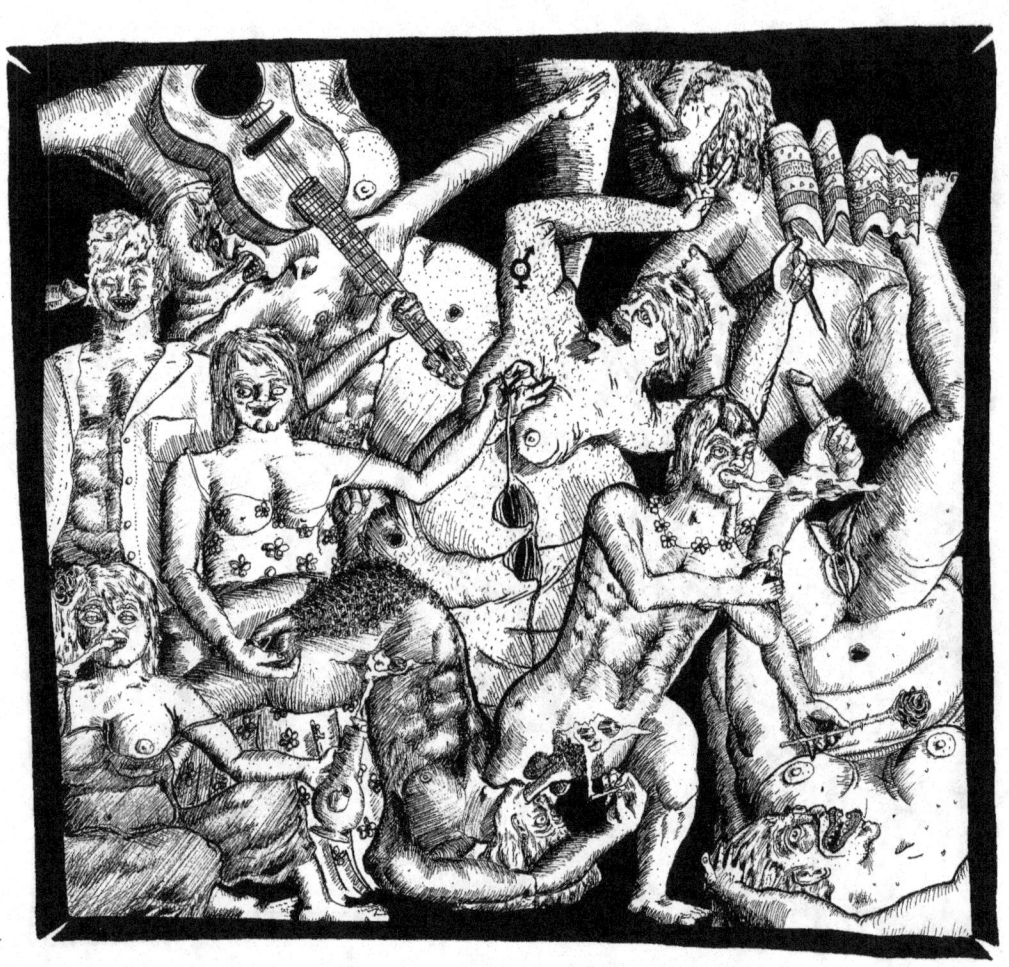

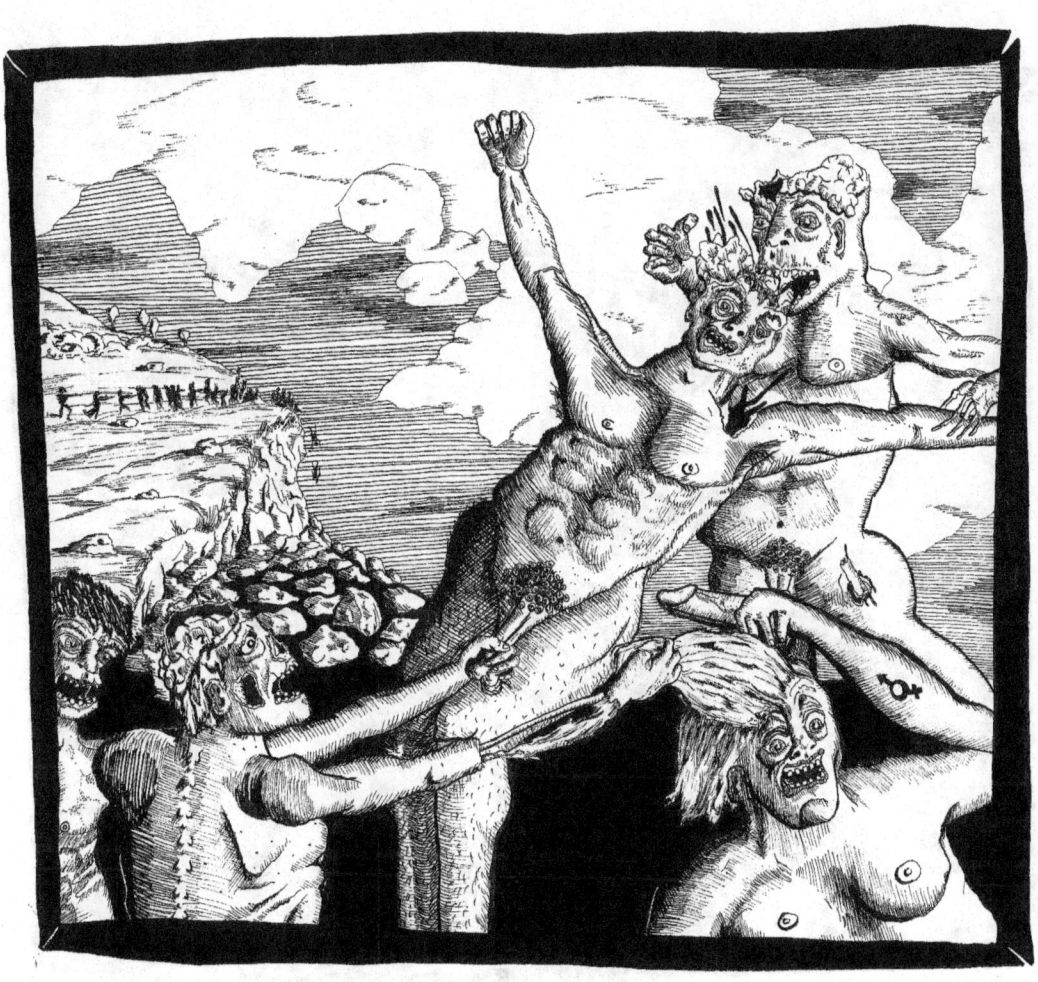

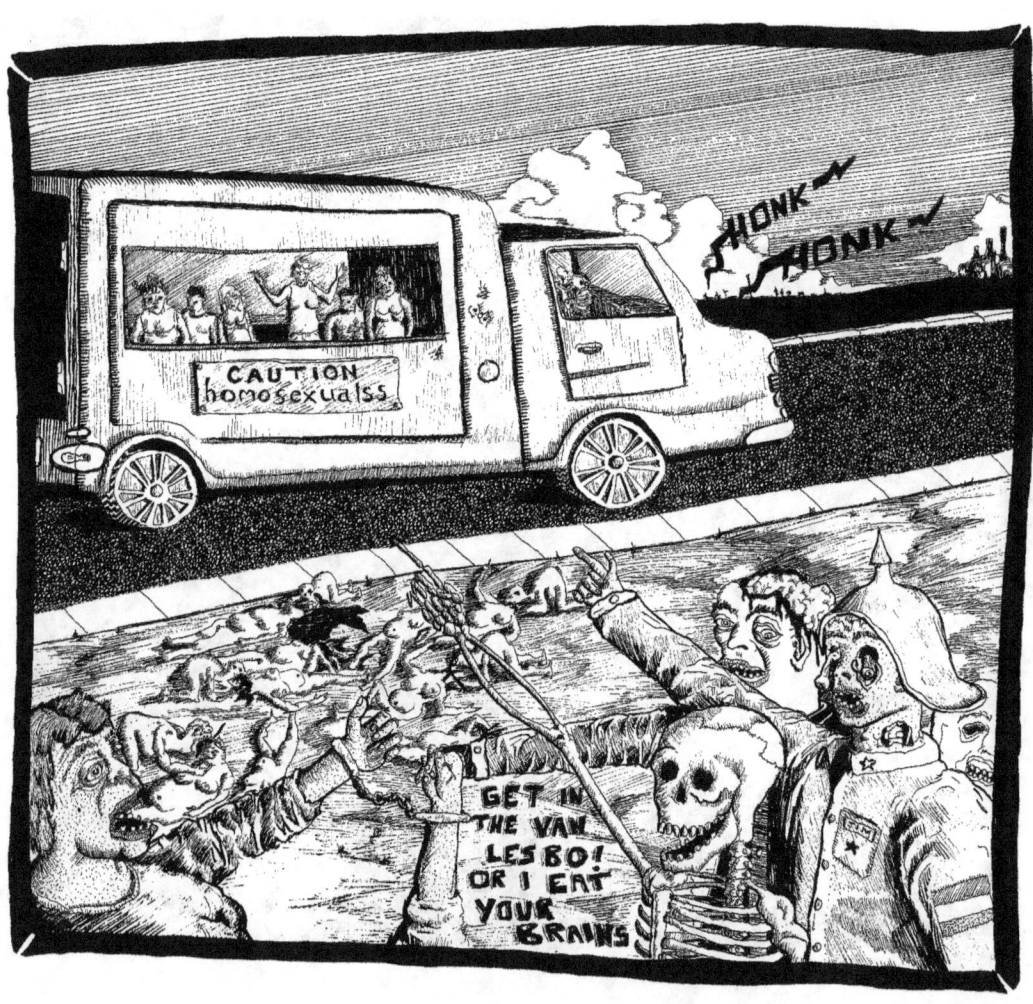

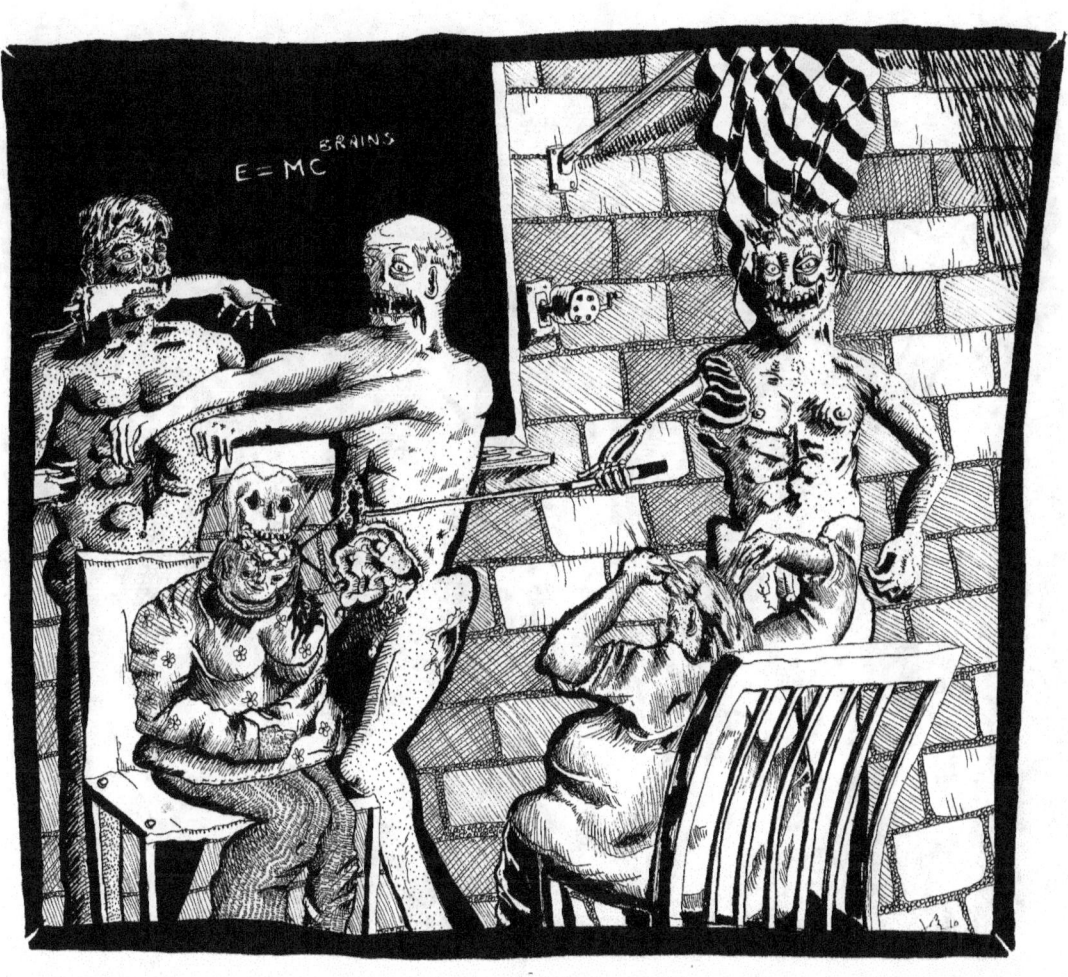

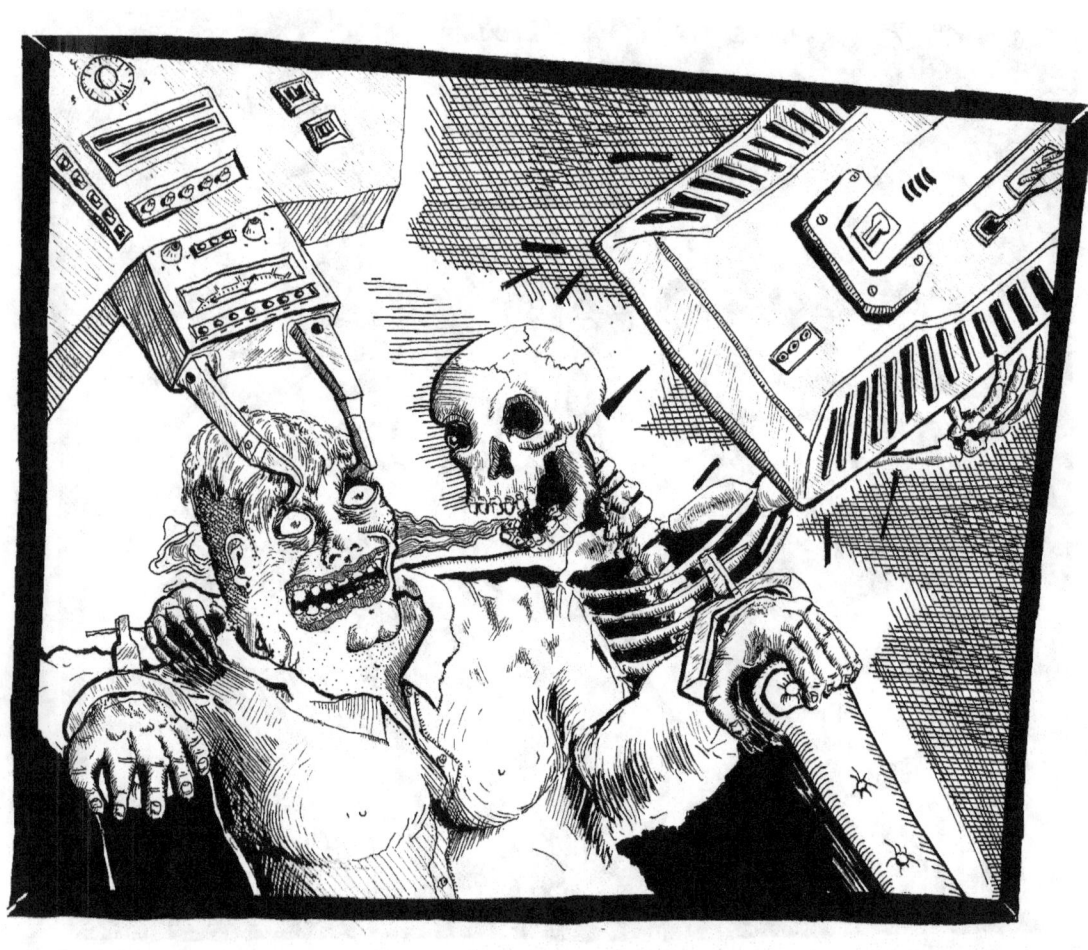

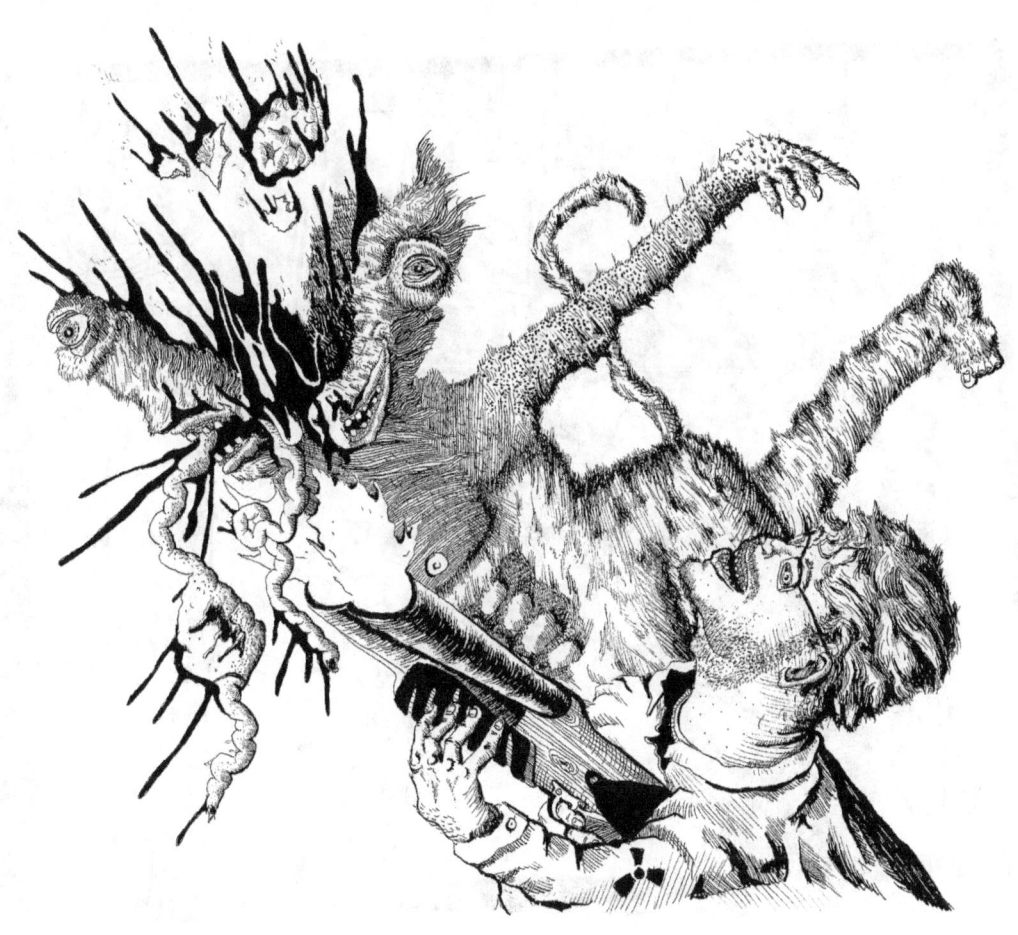

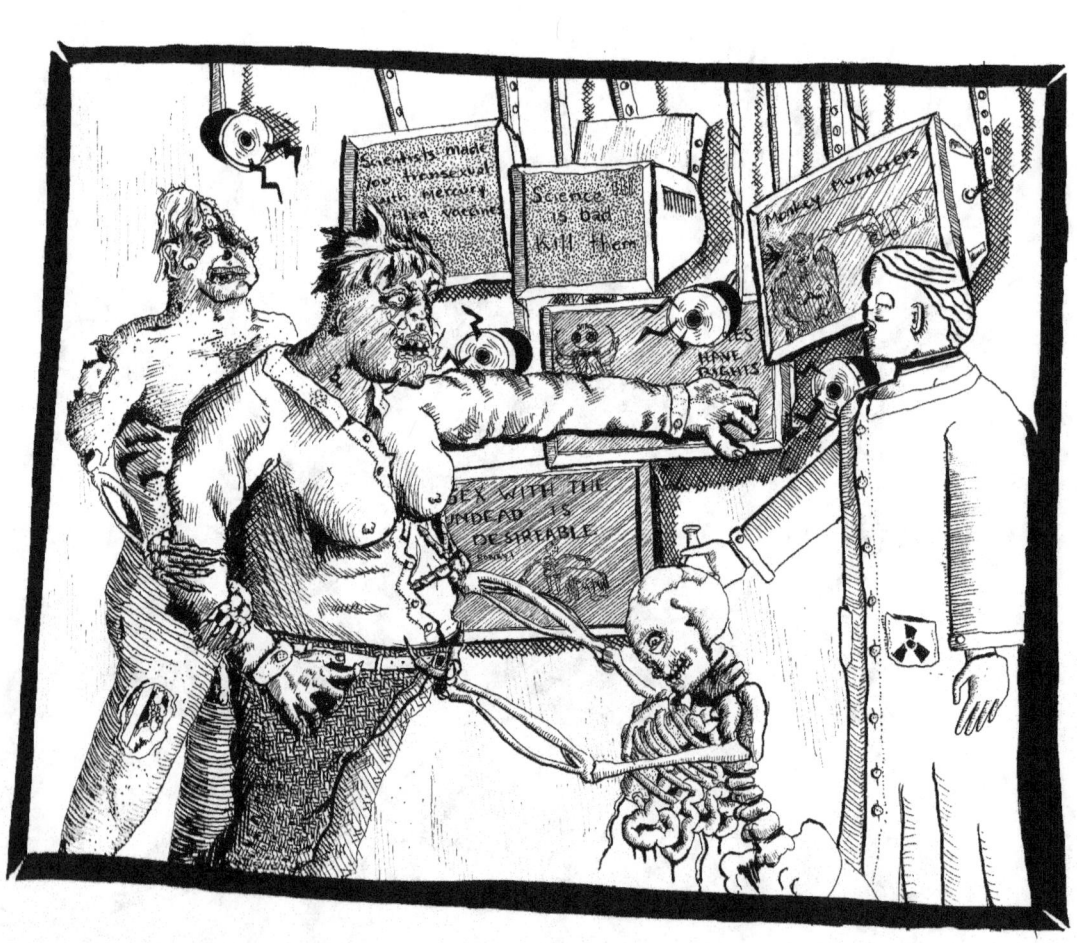

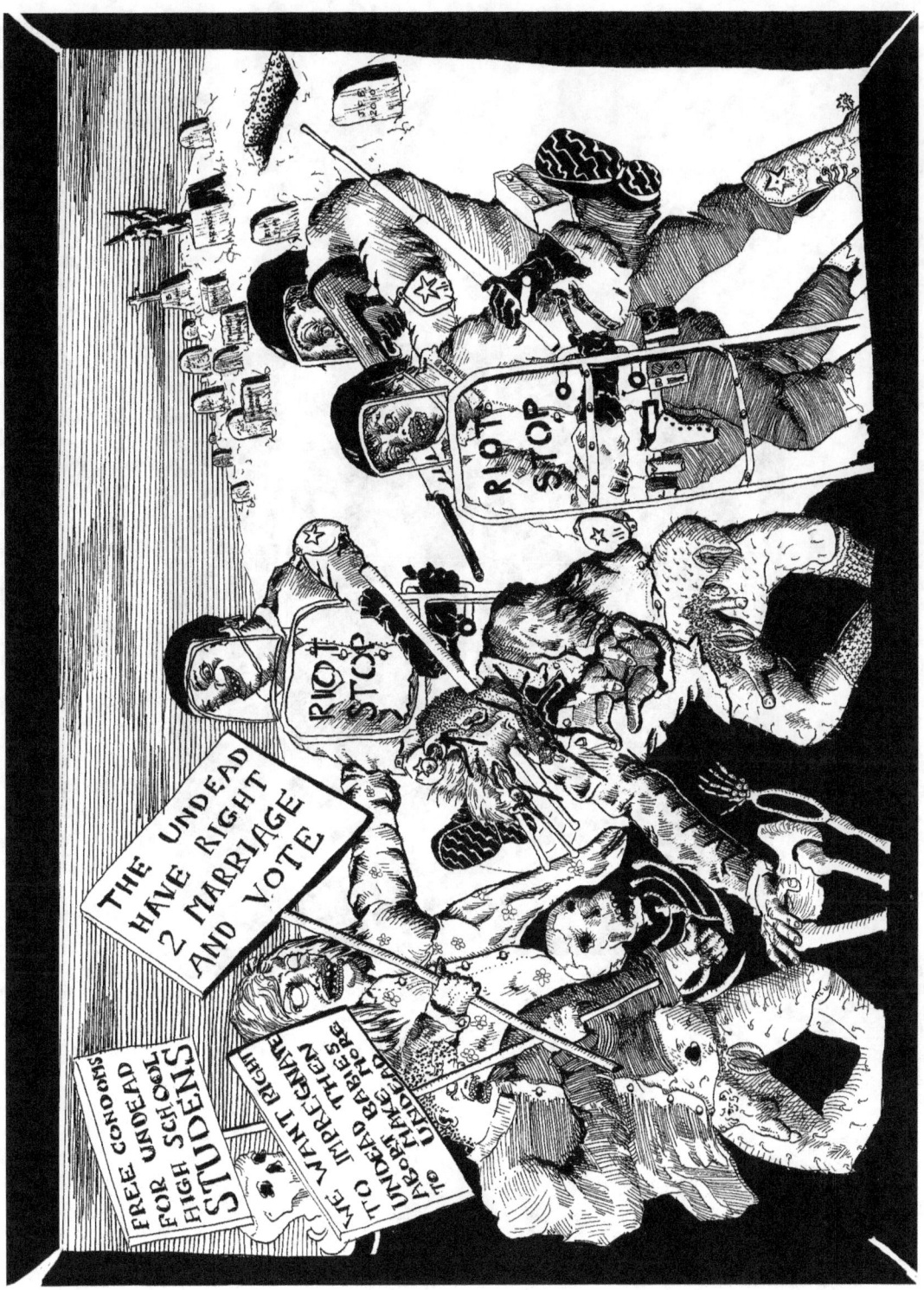

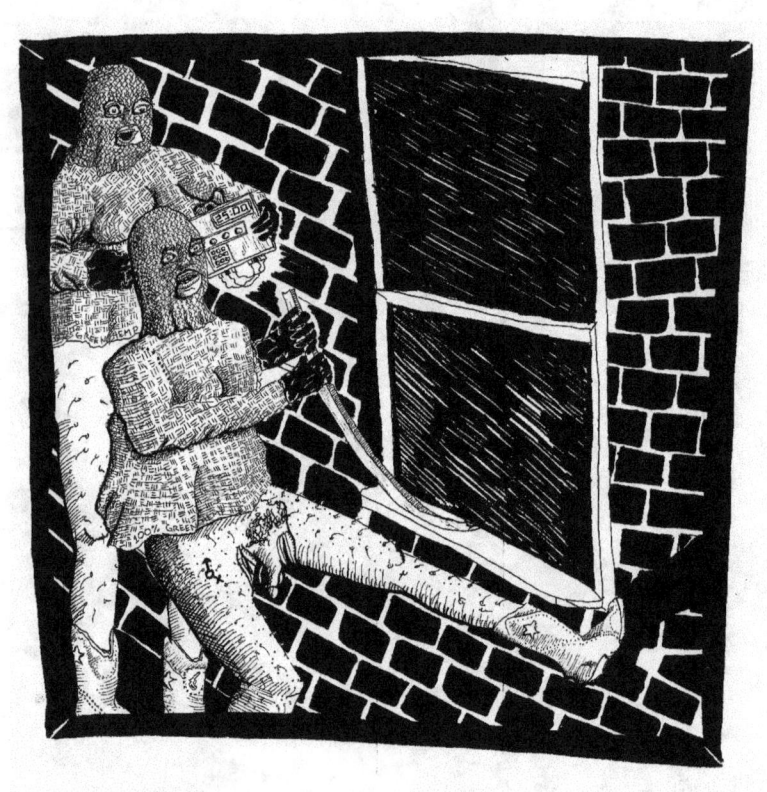

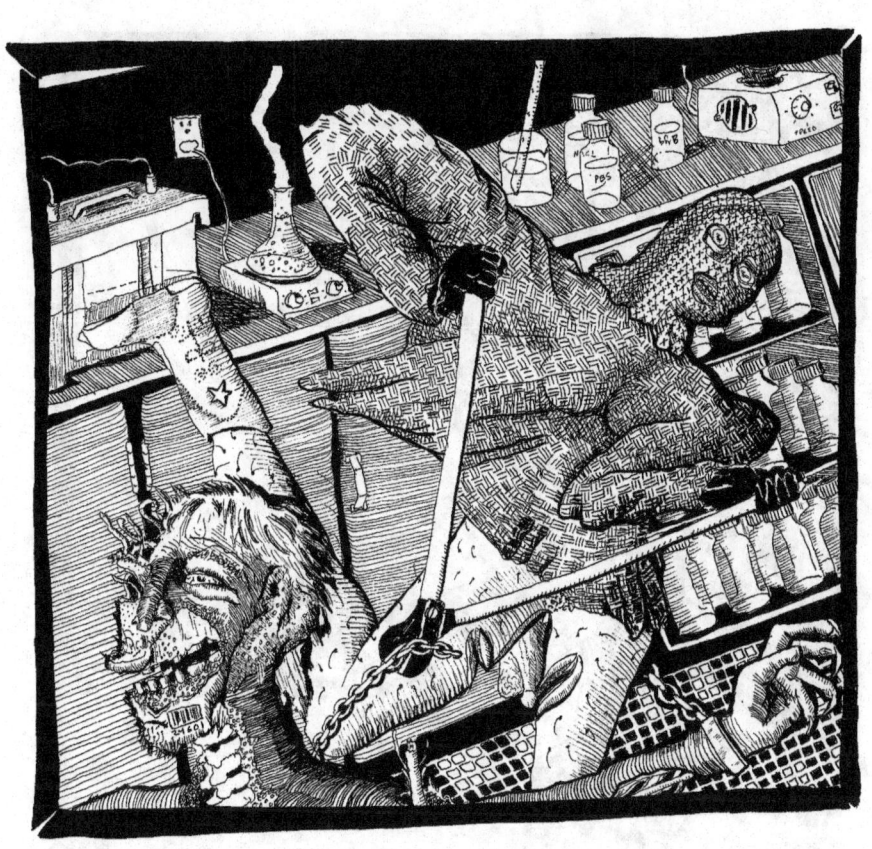

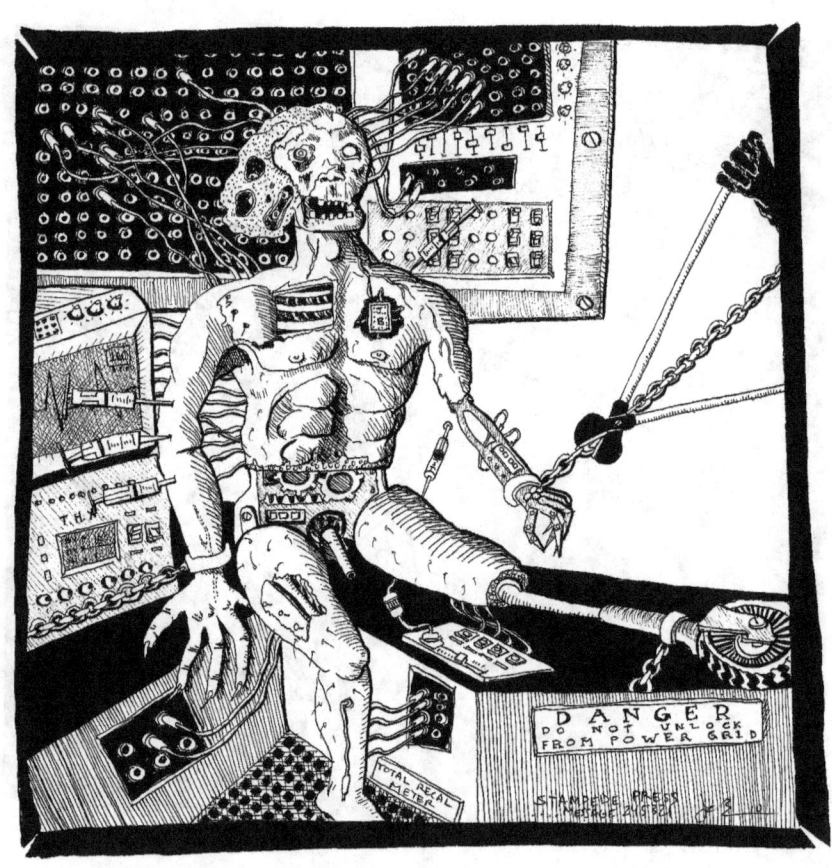

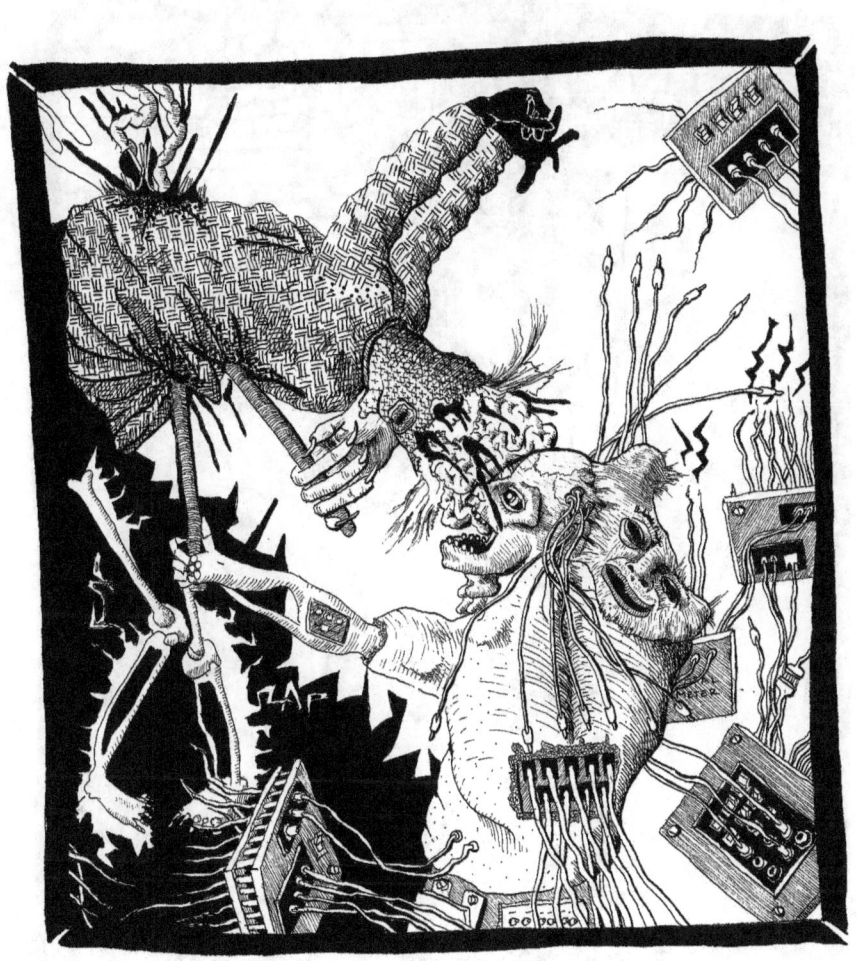

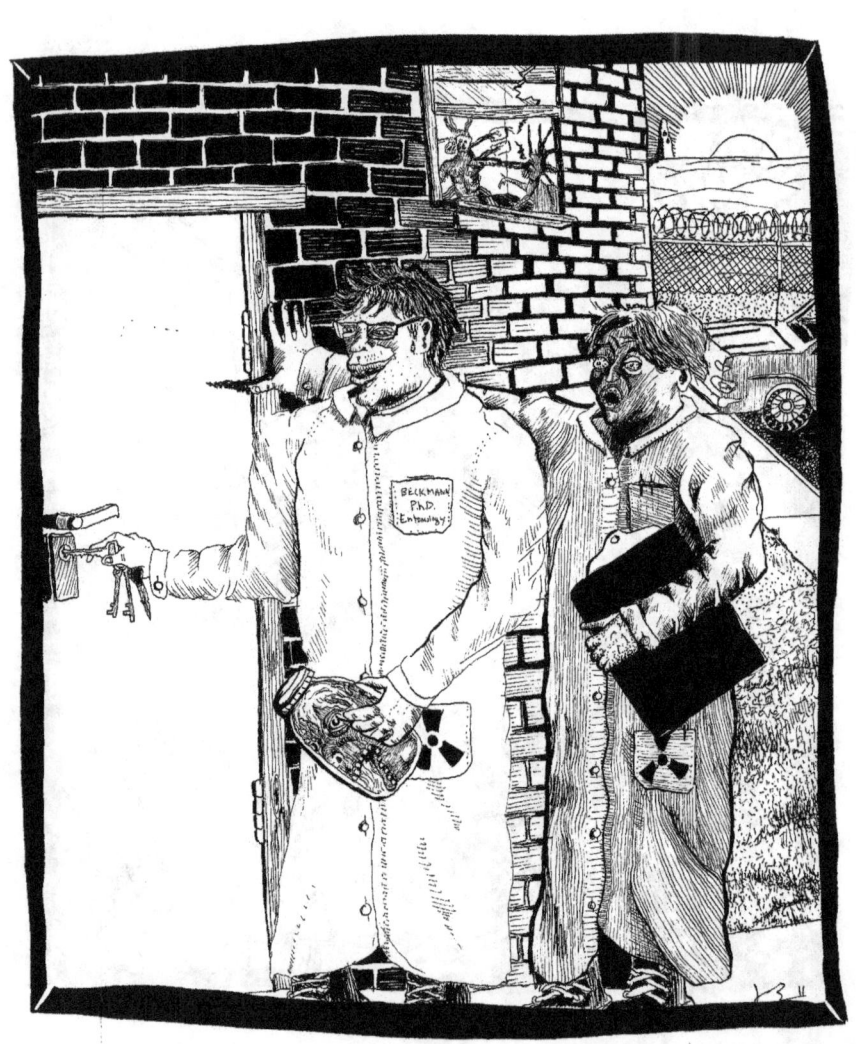

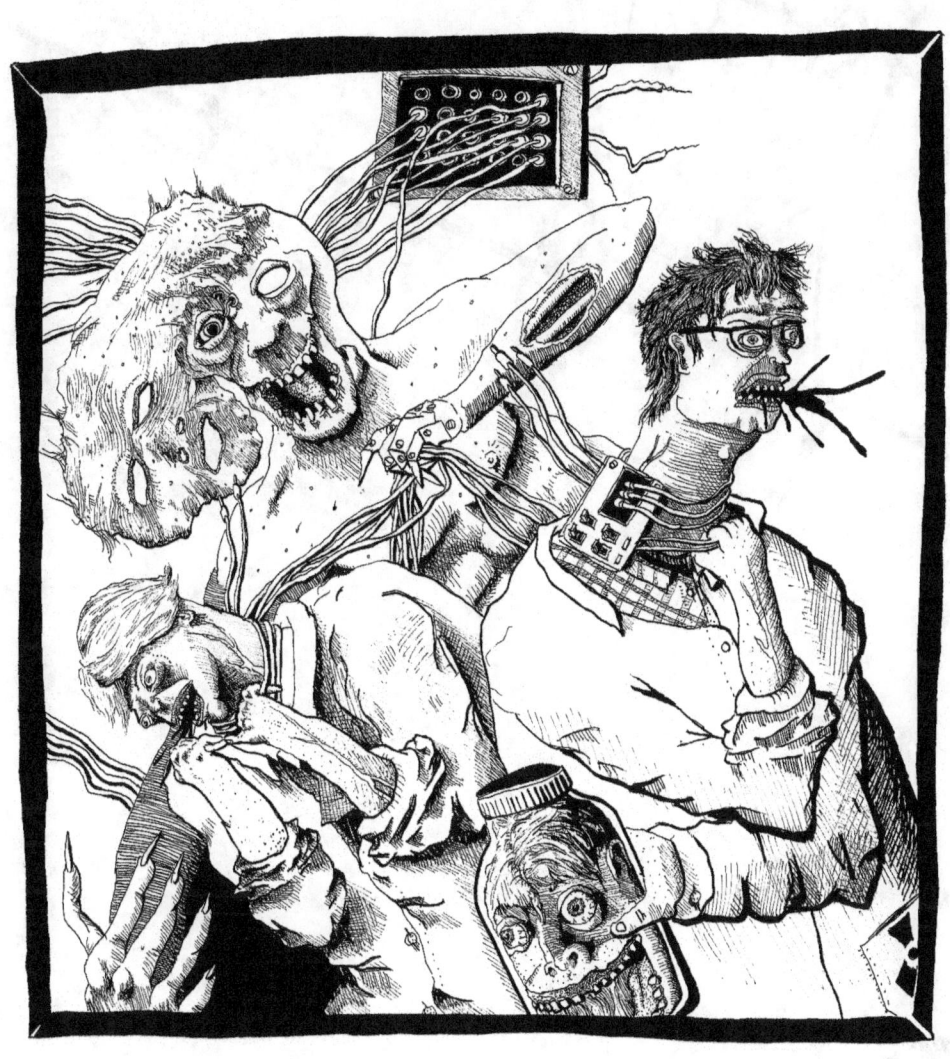

Portfolio 6

Kuato Lives

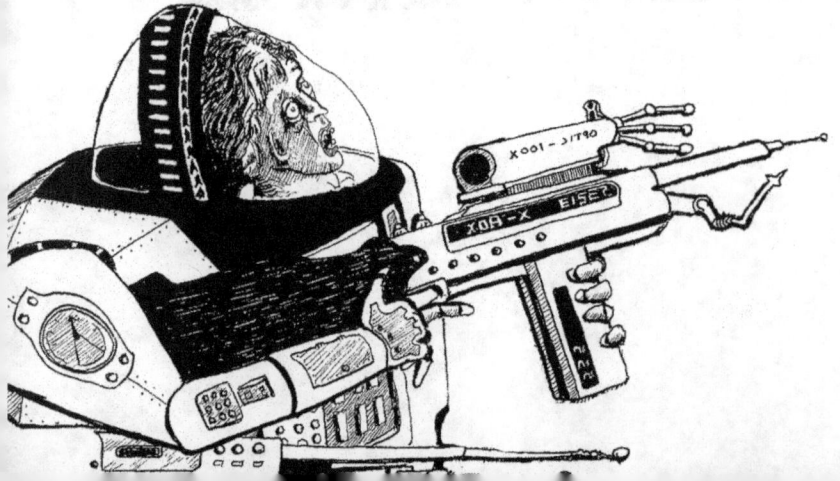

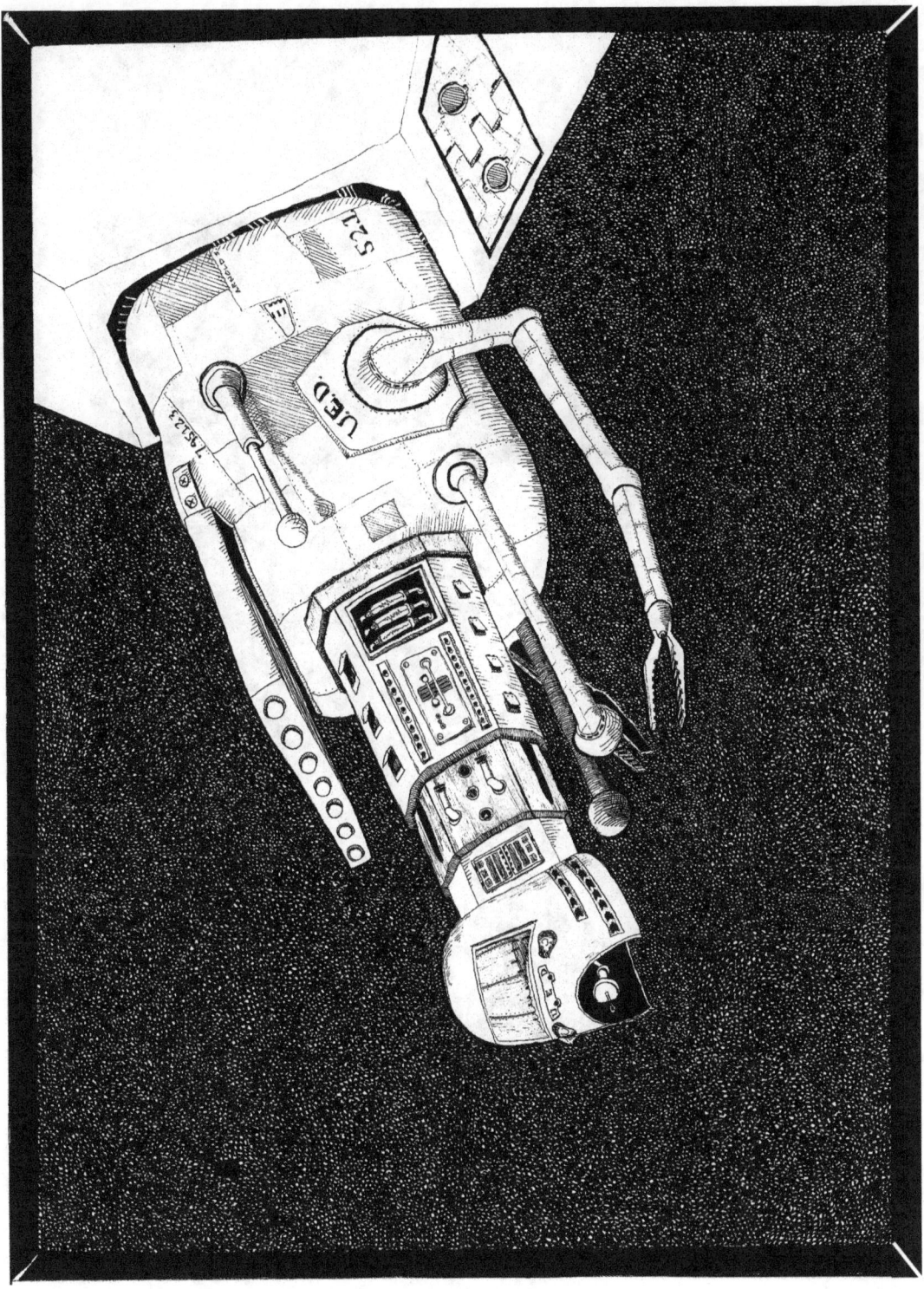

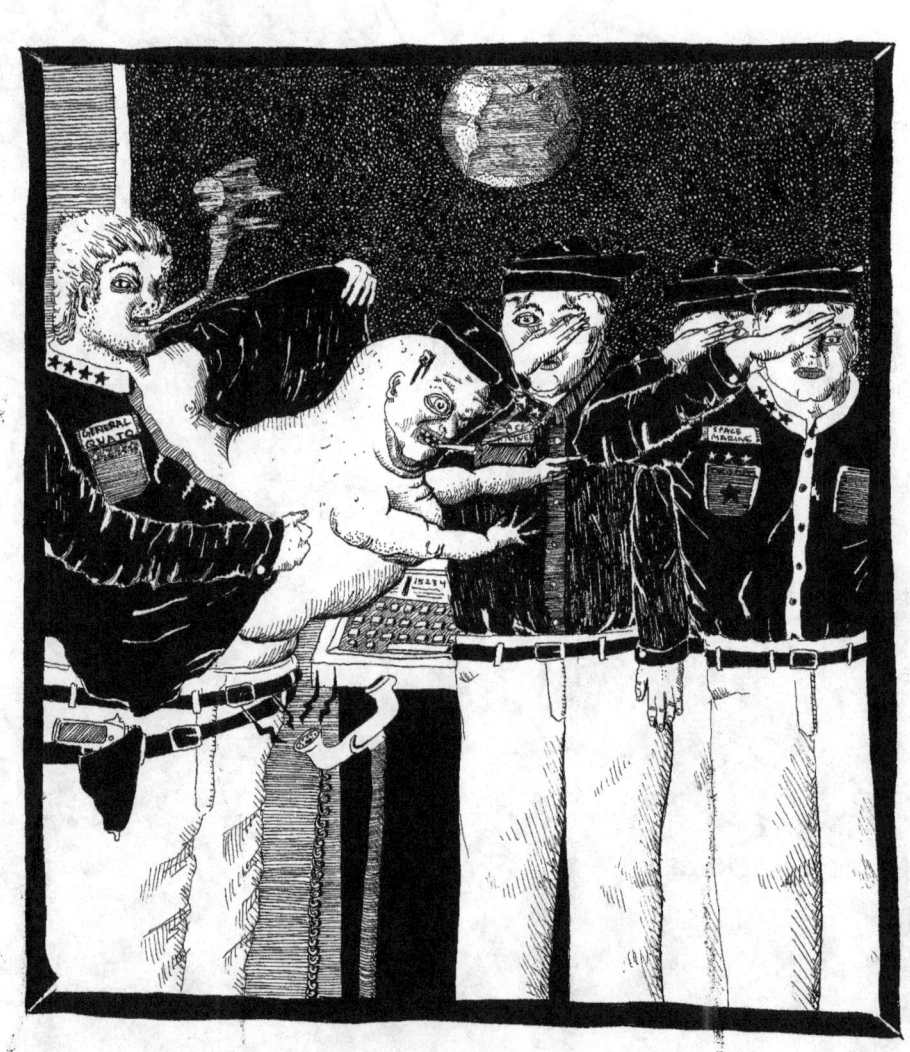

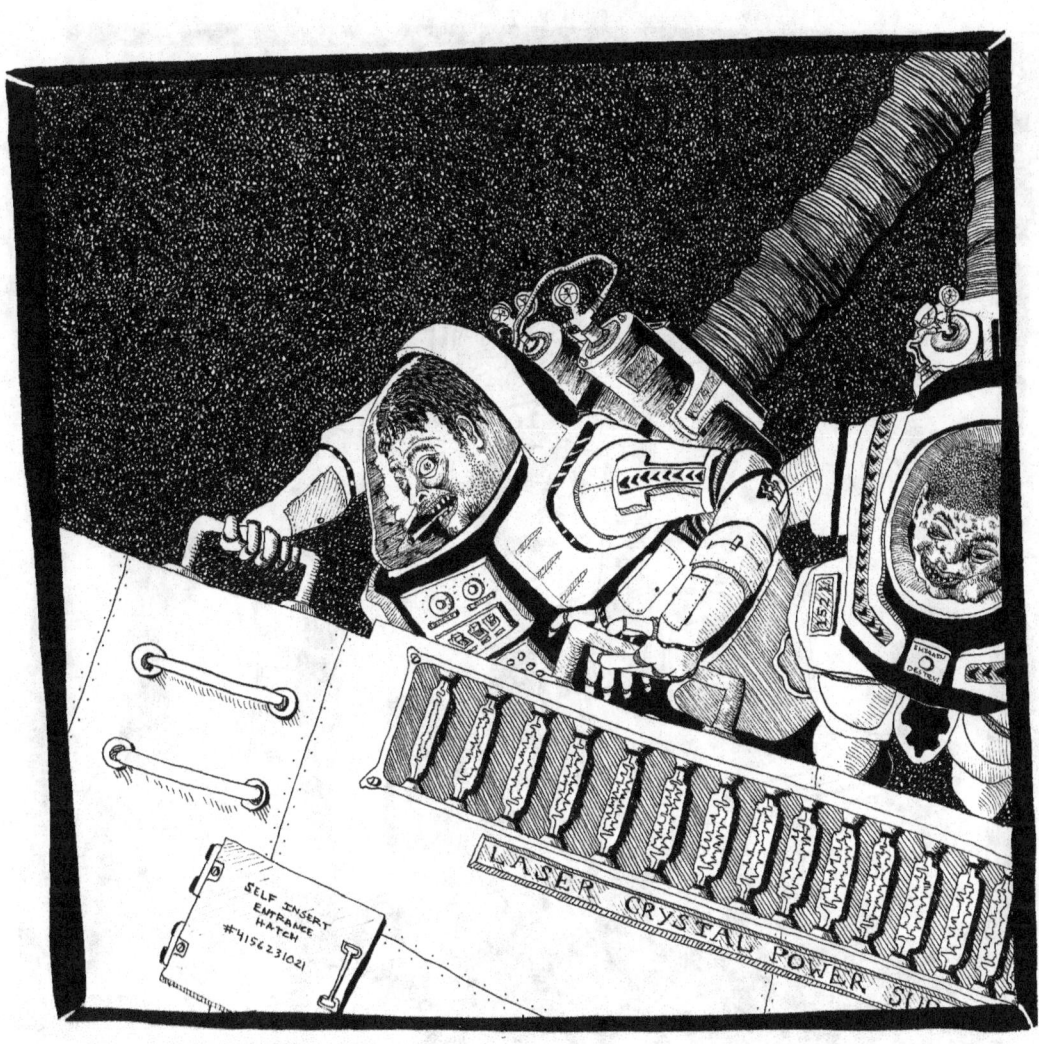

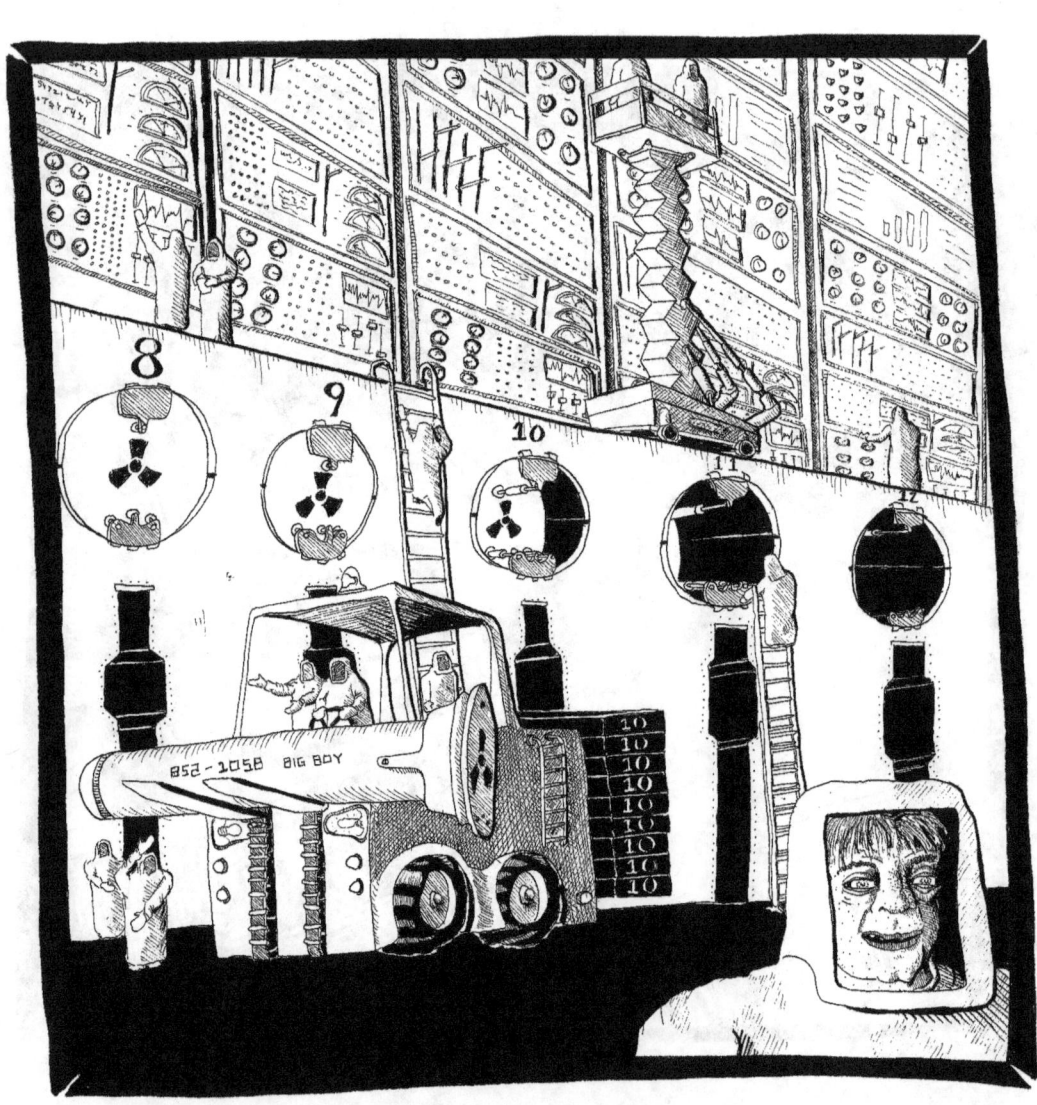

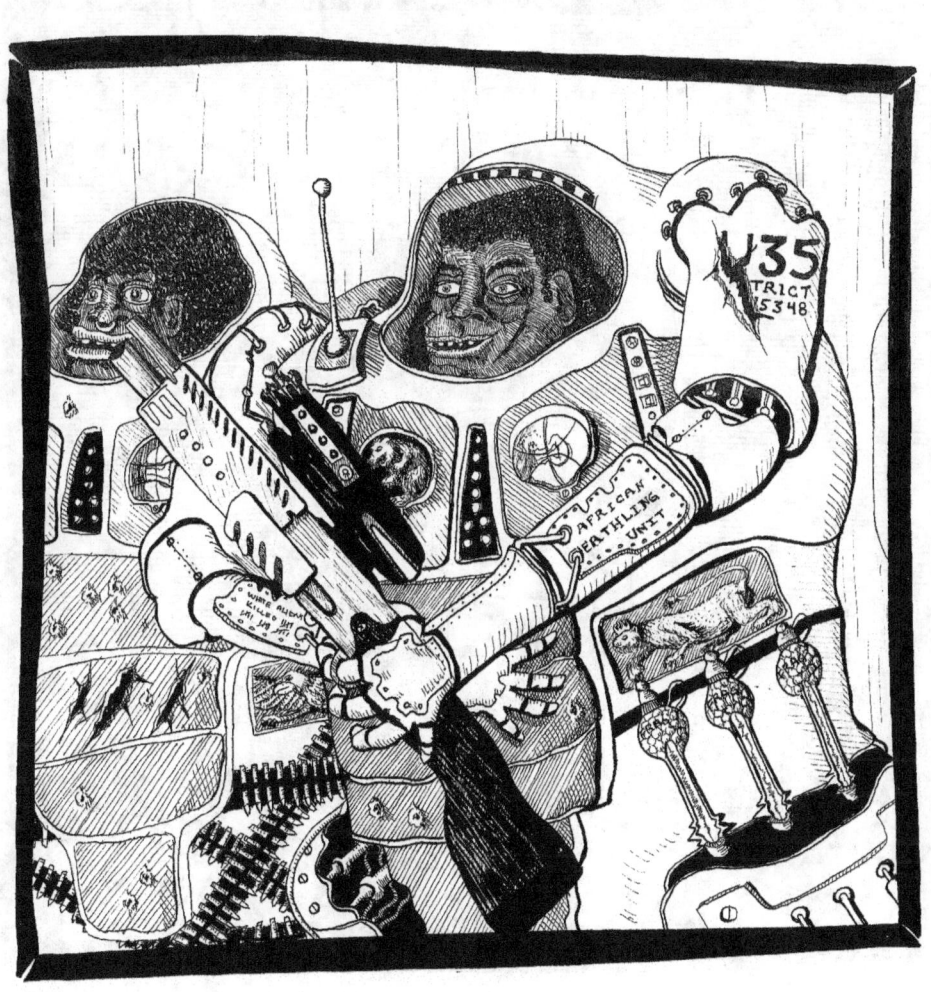

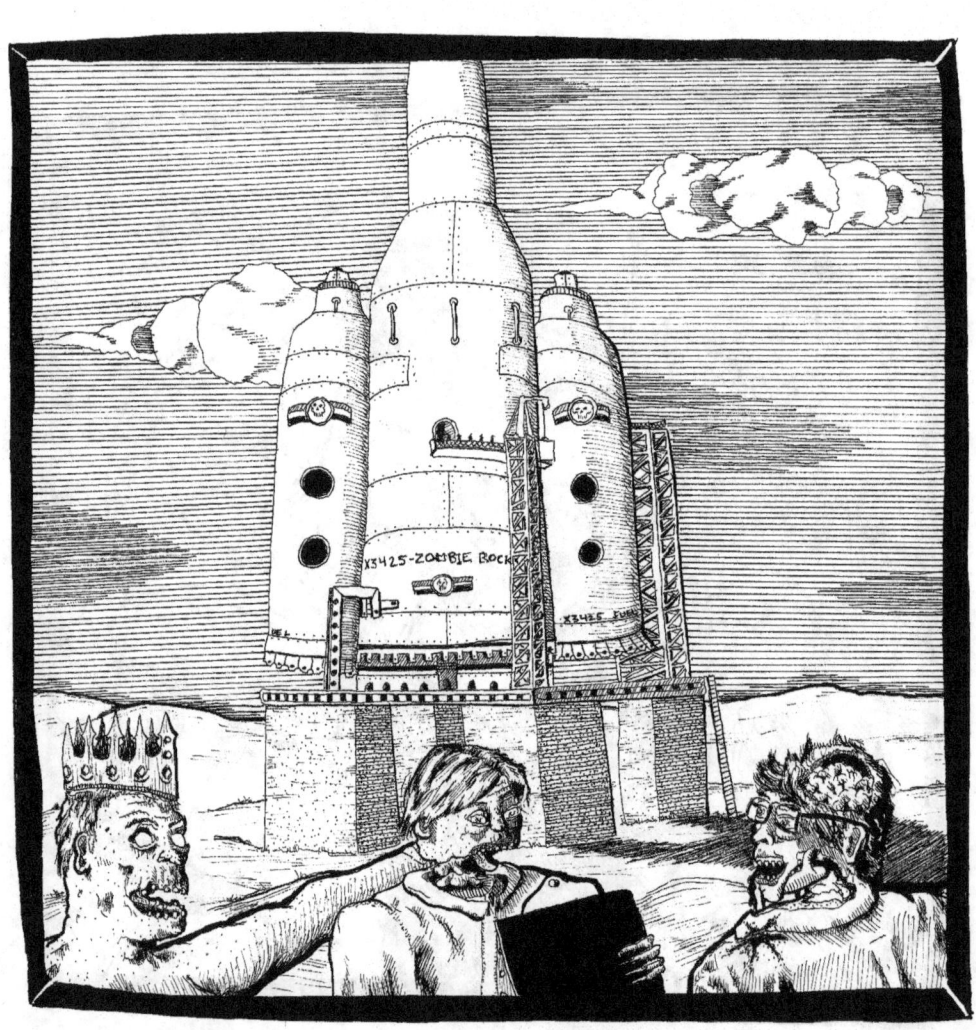

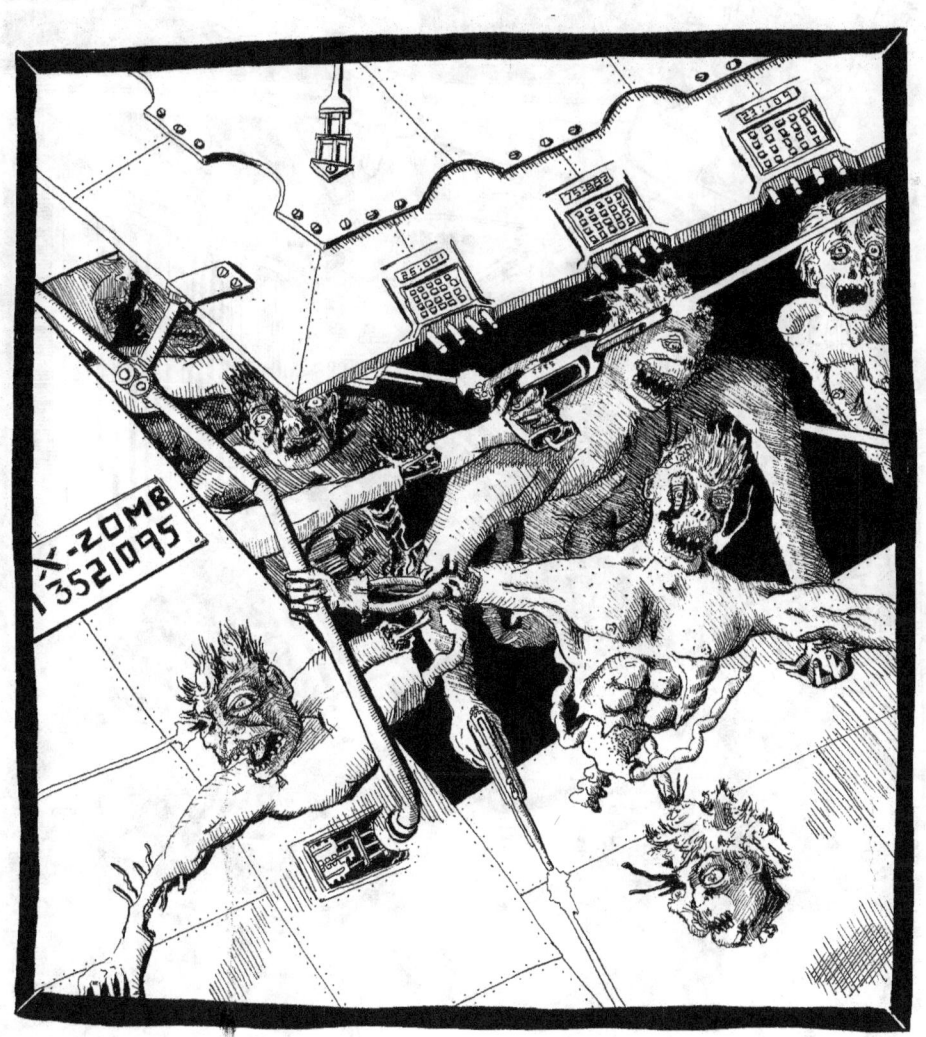

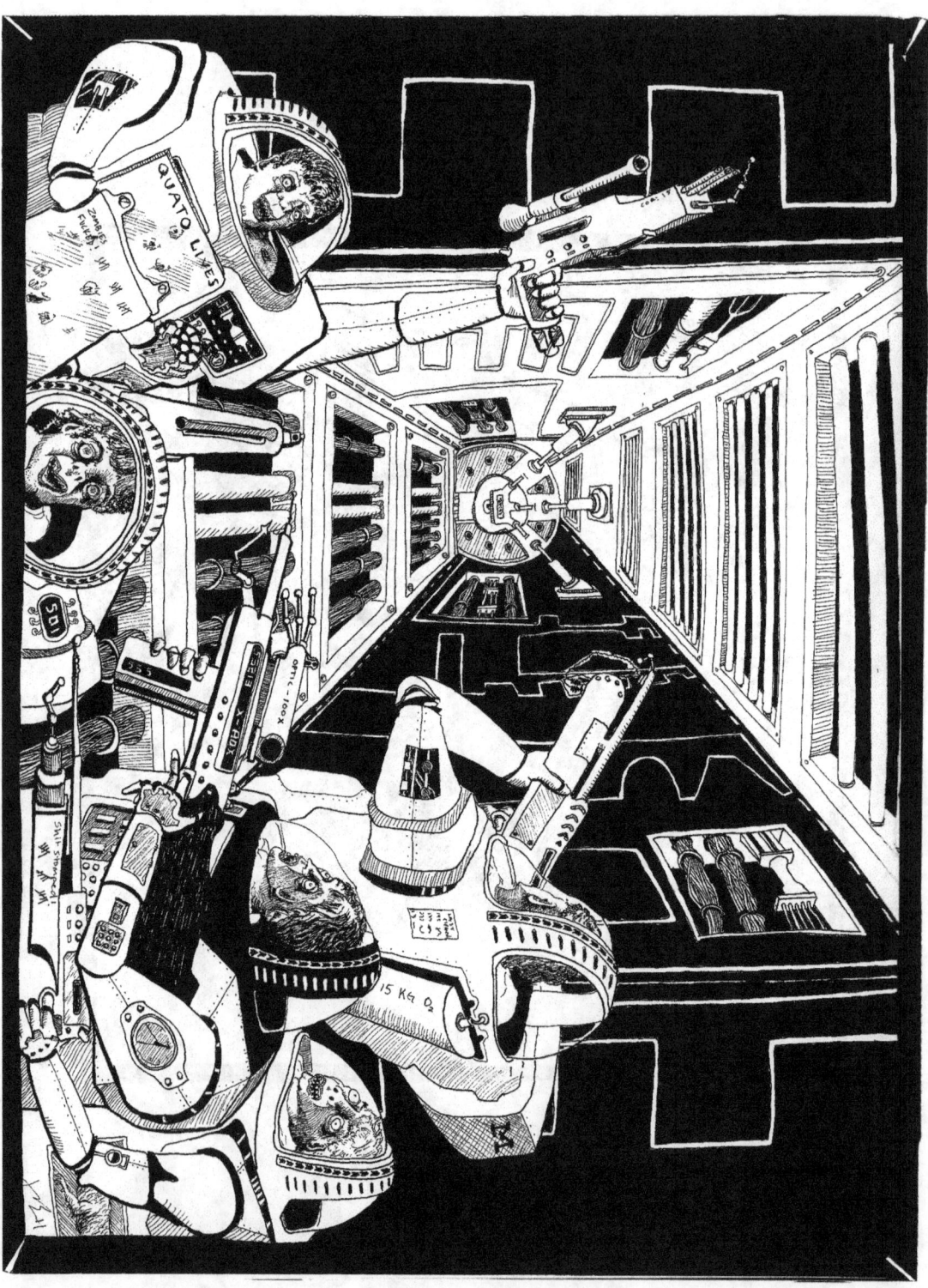

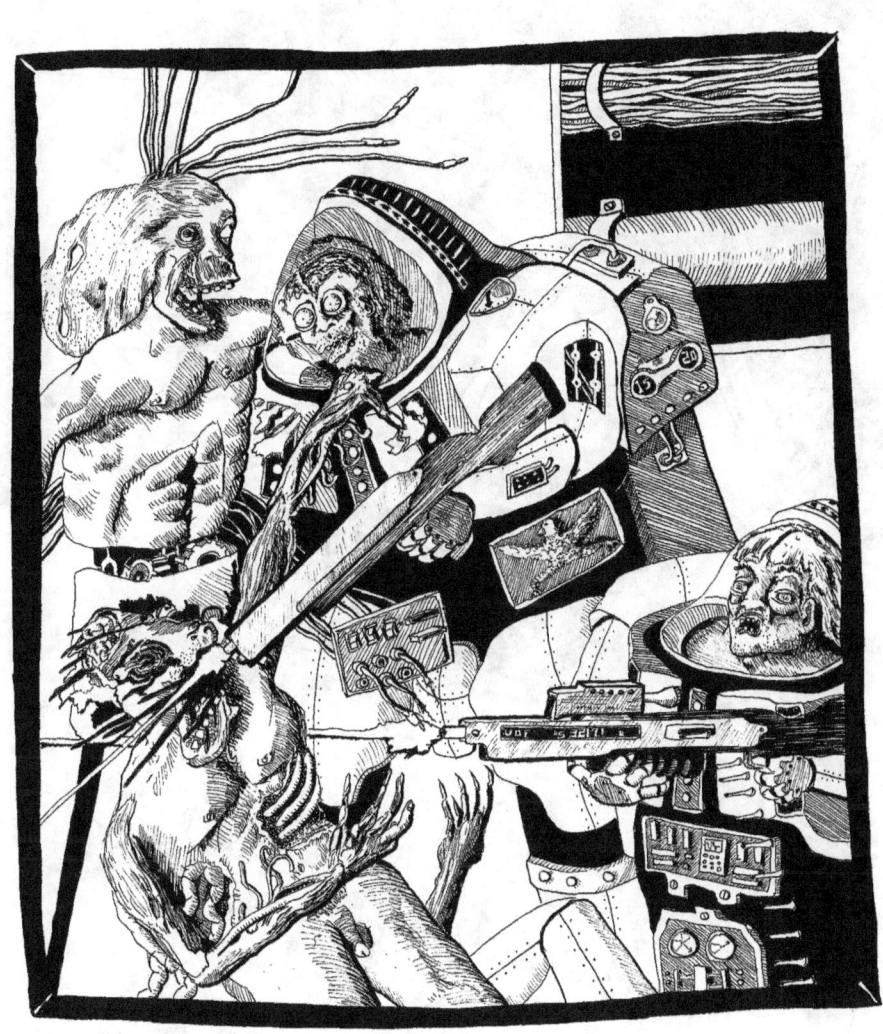

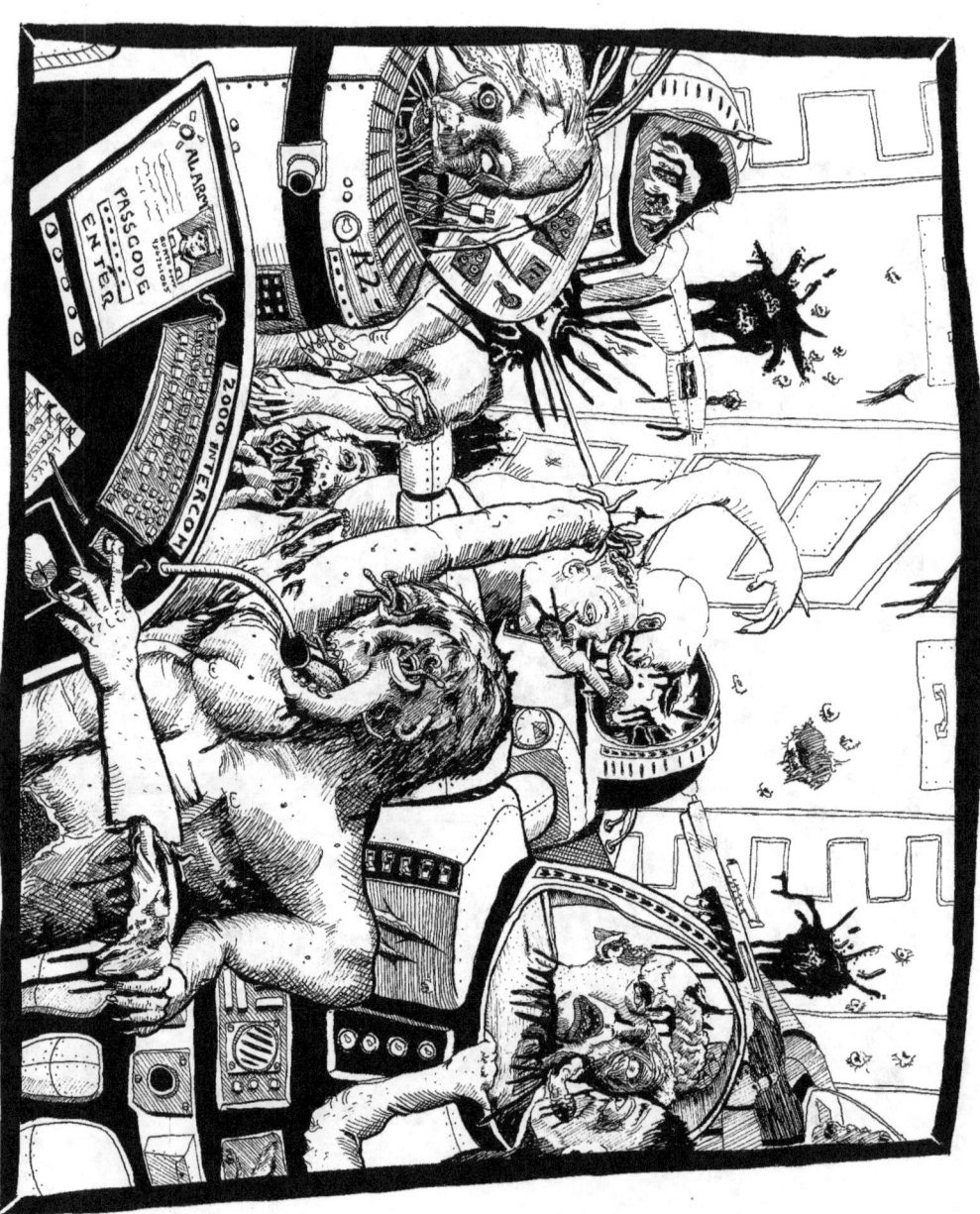

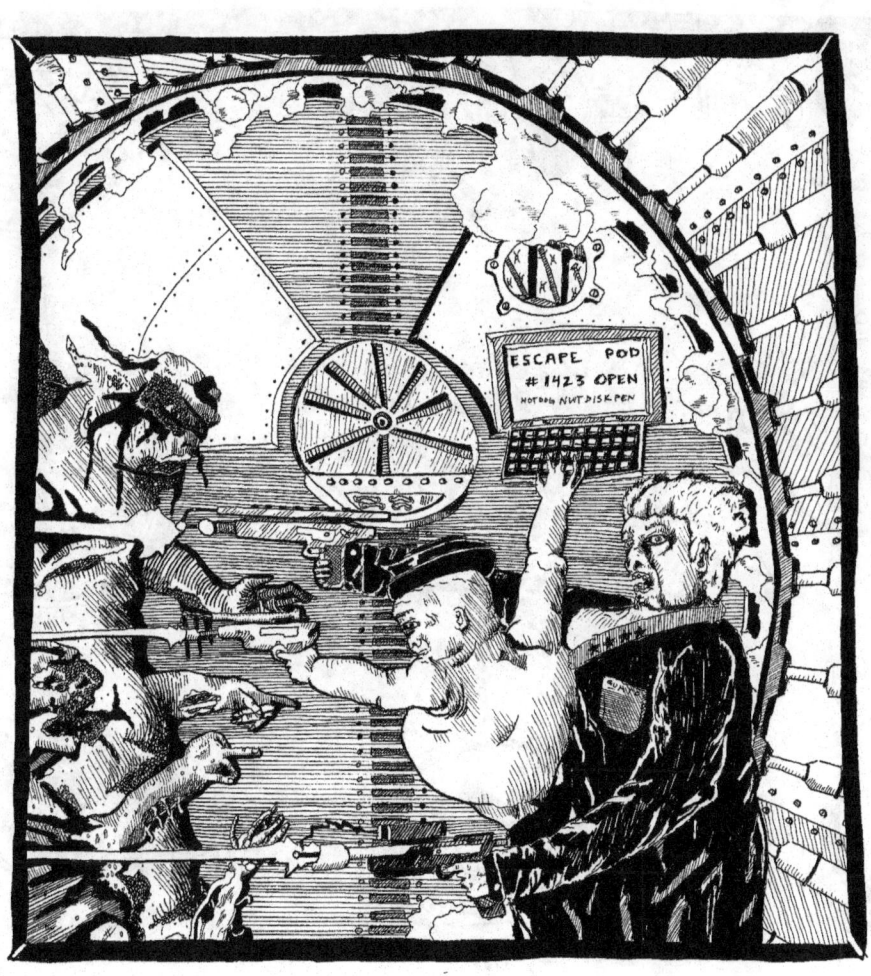

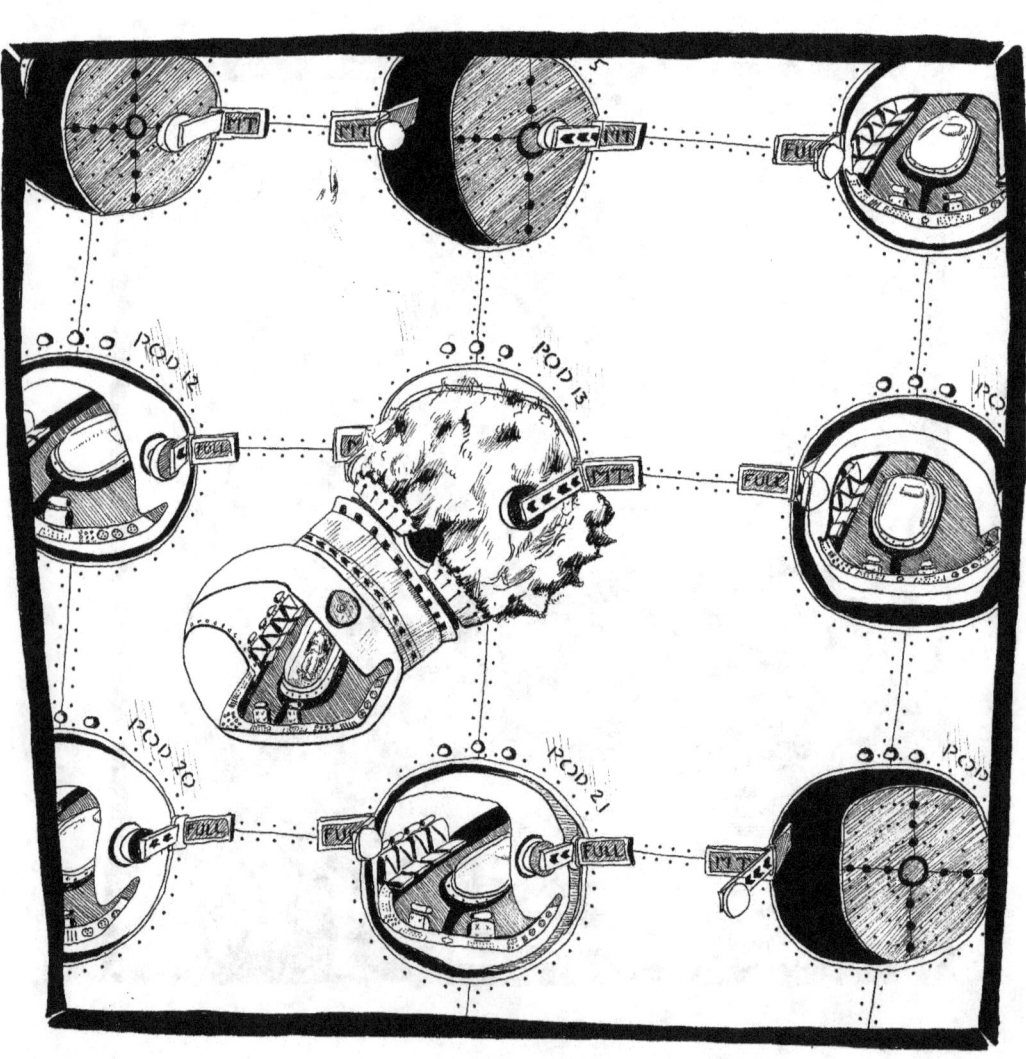

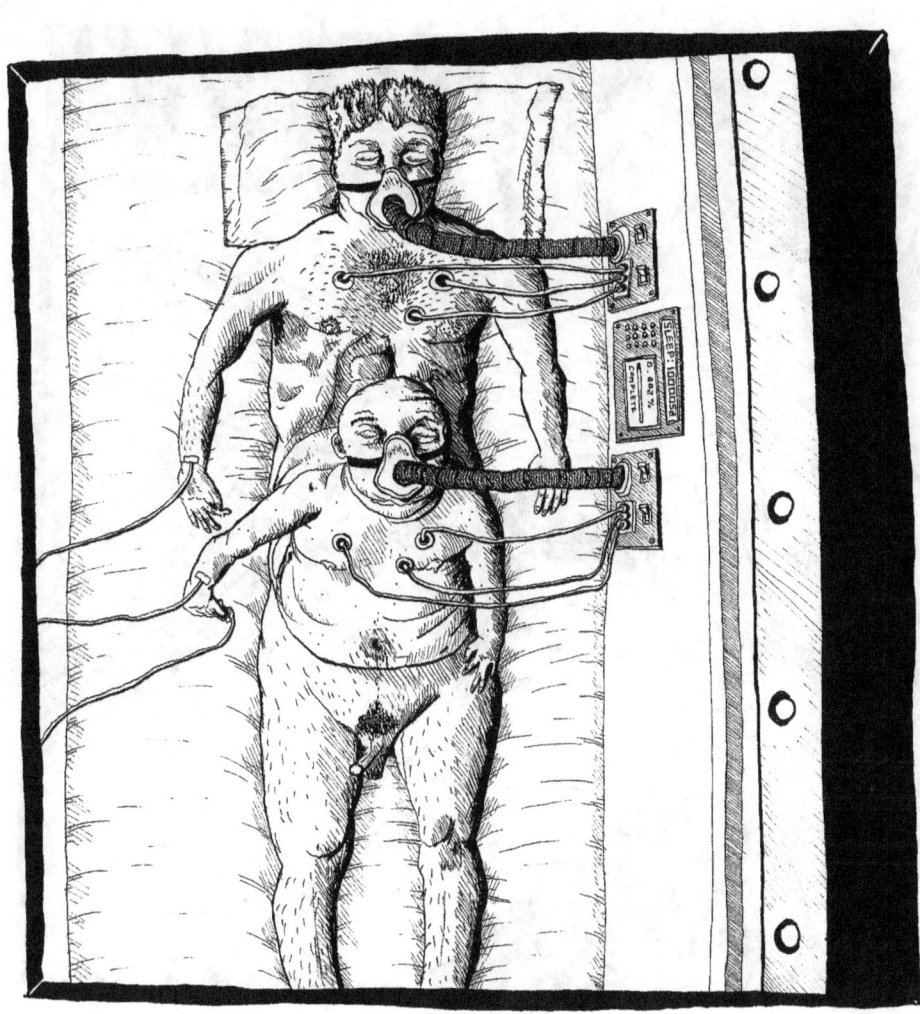

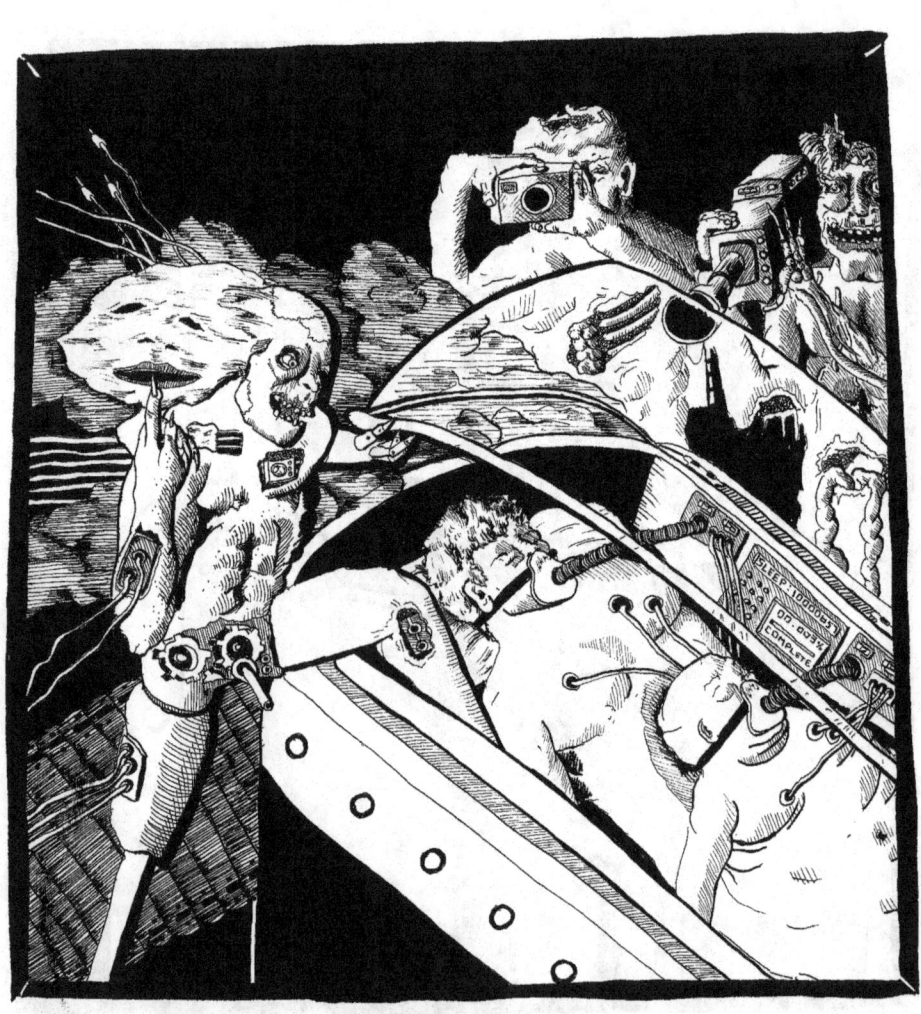

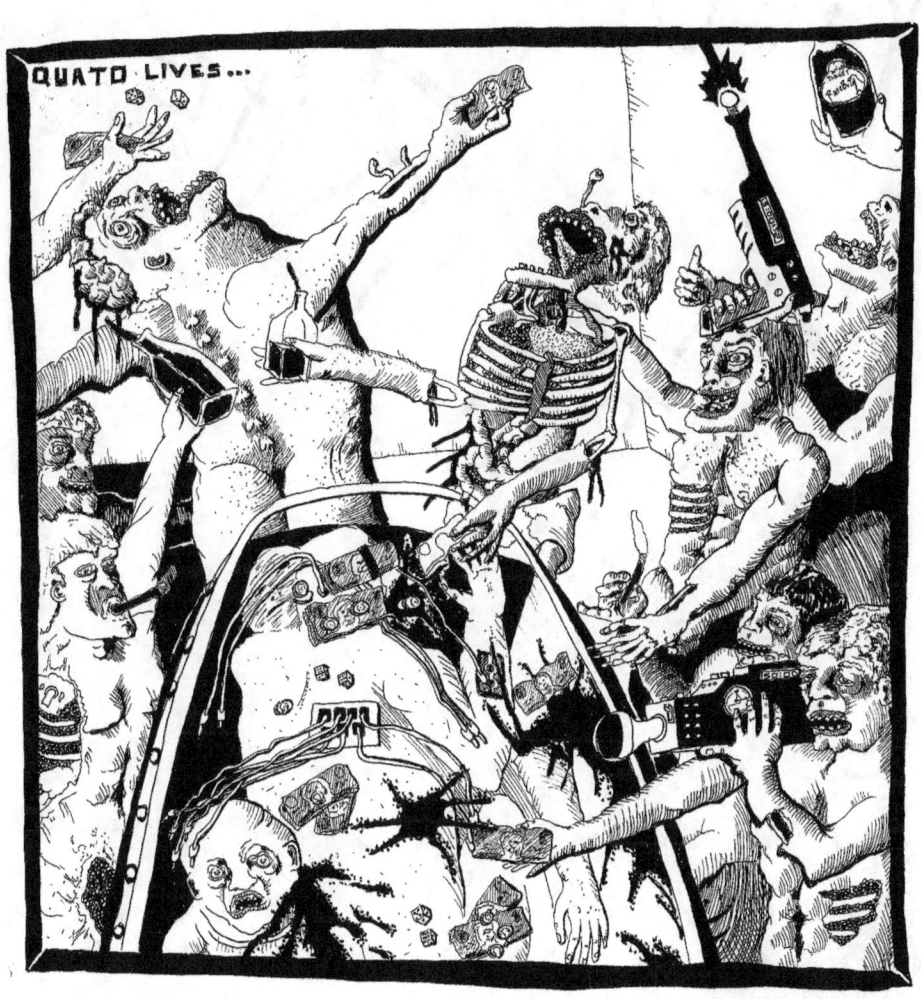

Portfolio 7

The Rite

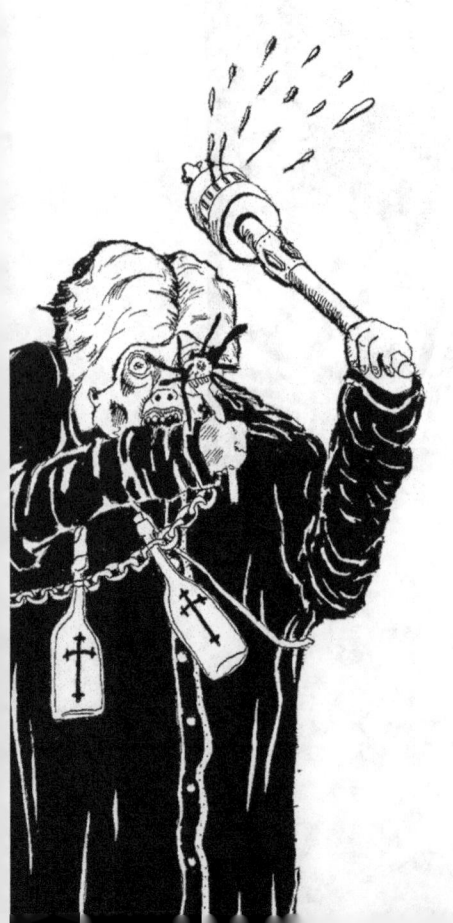

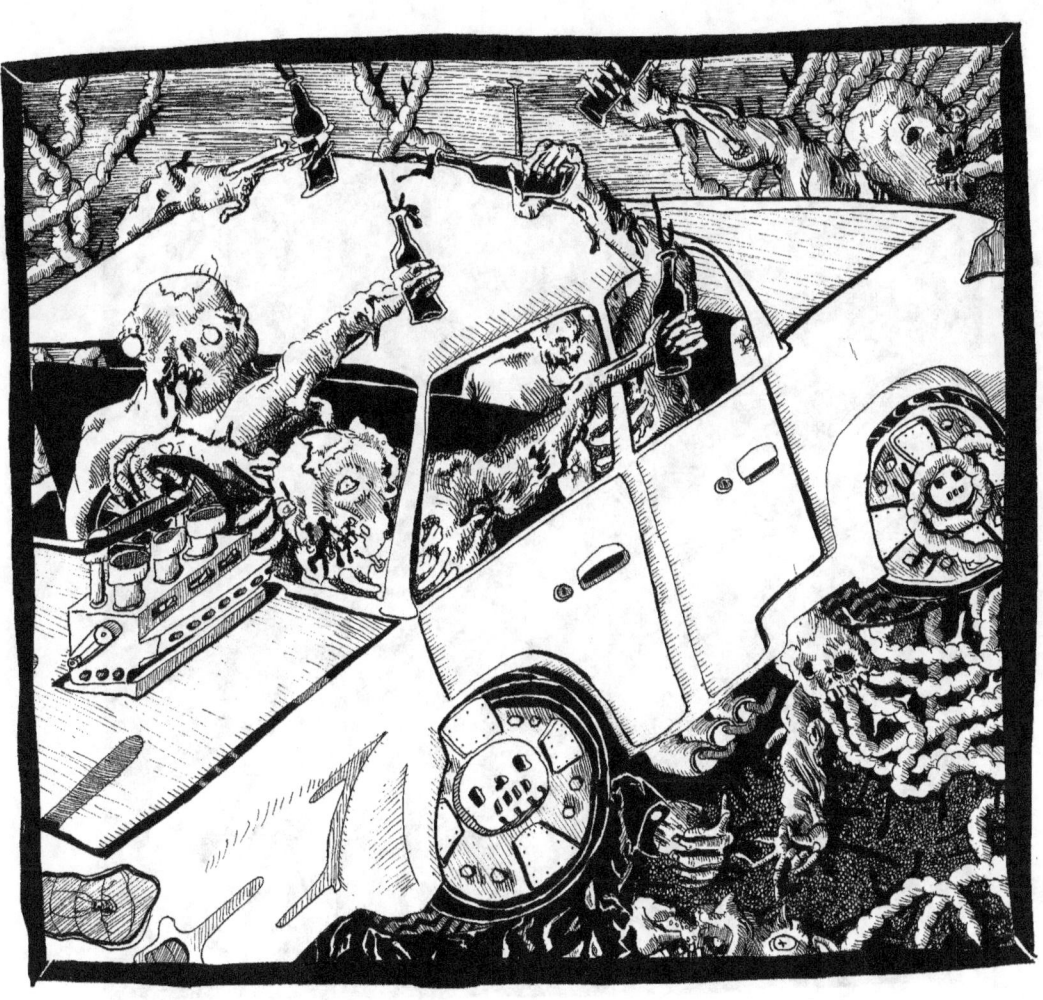

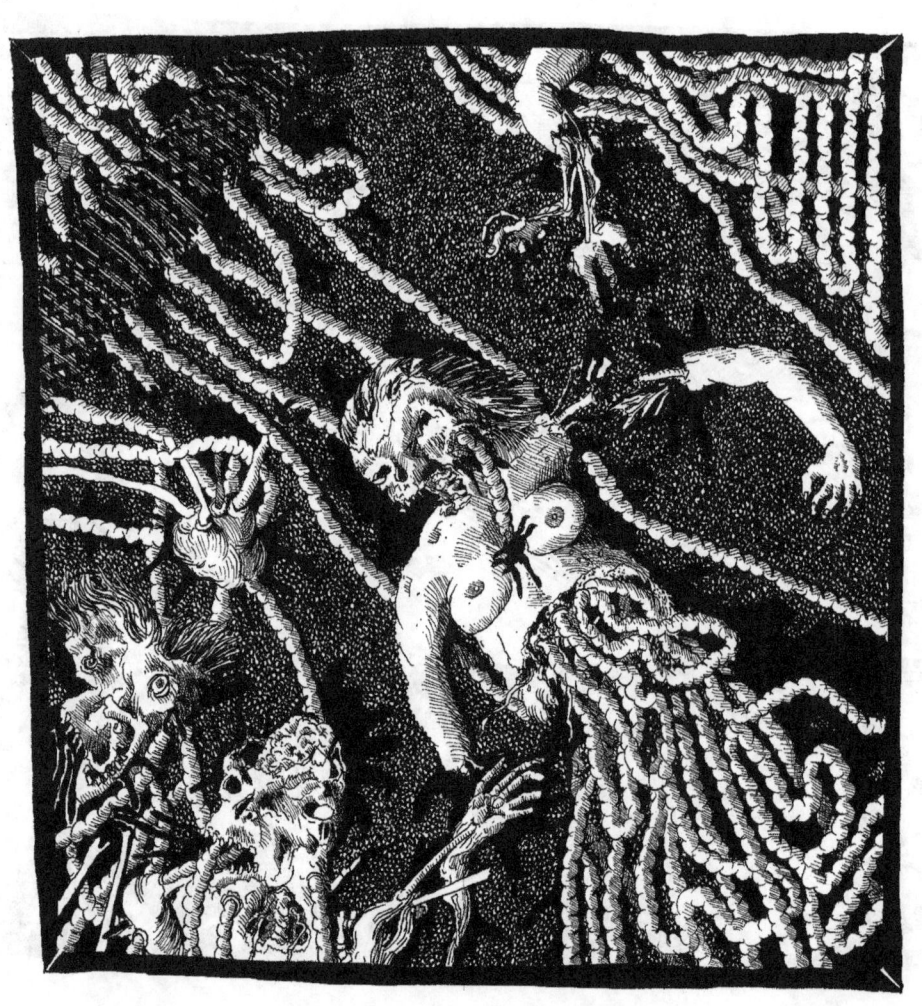

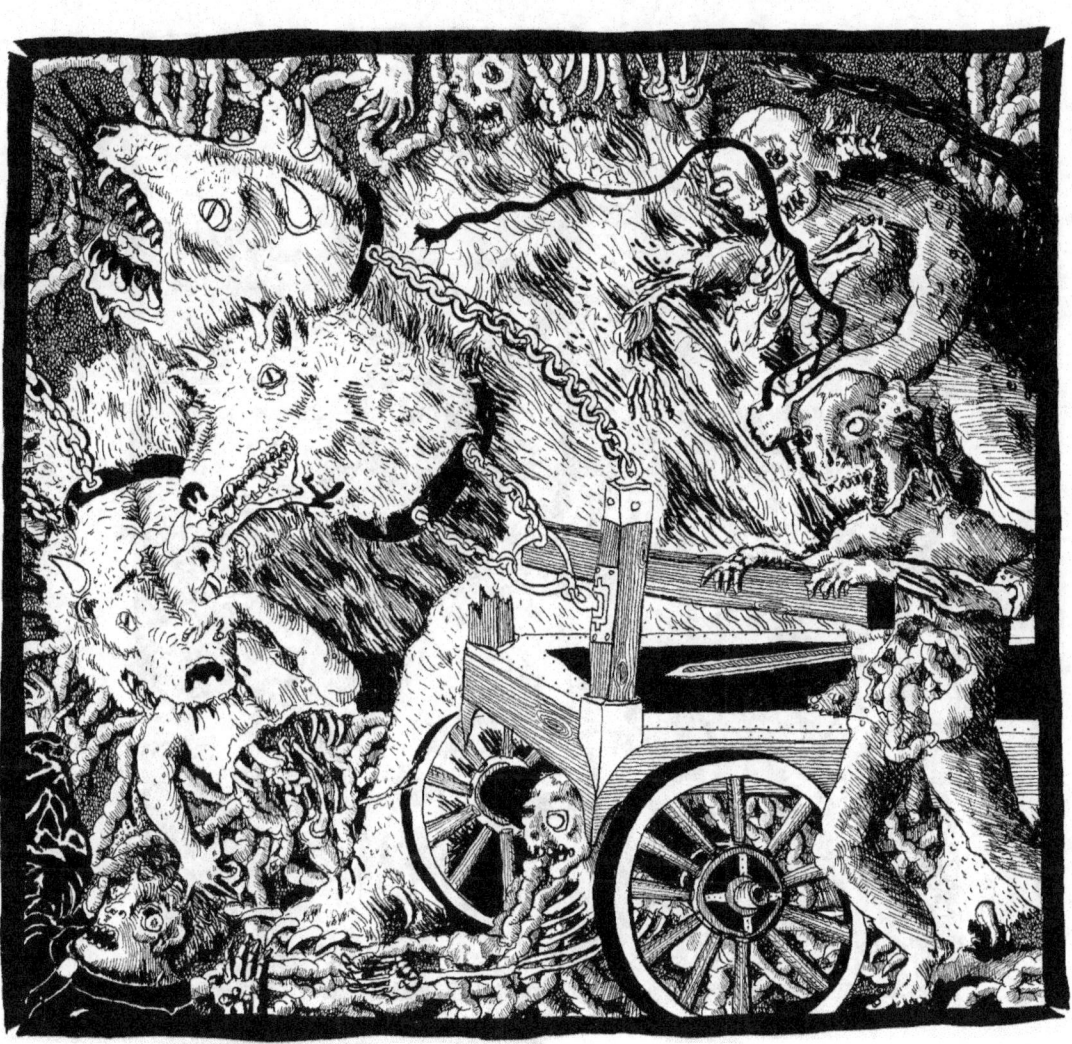

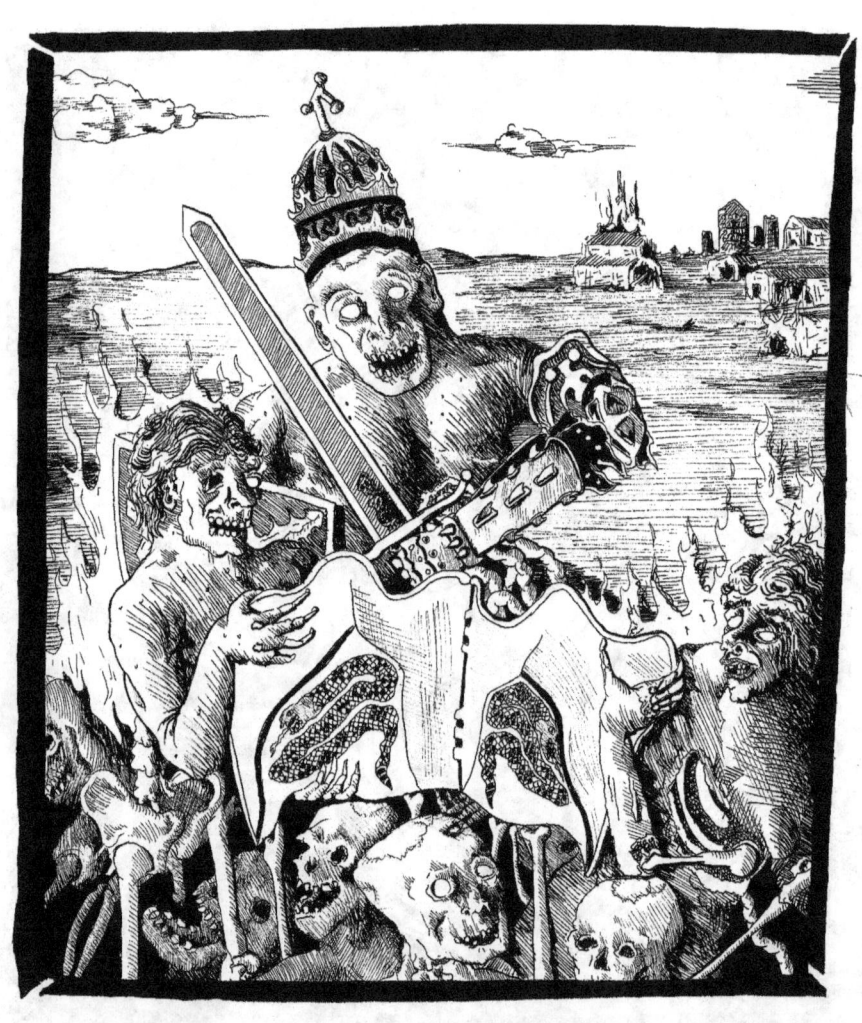

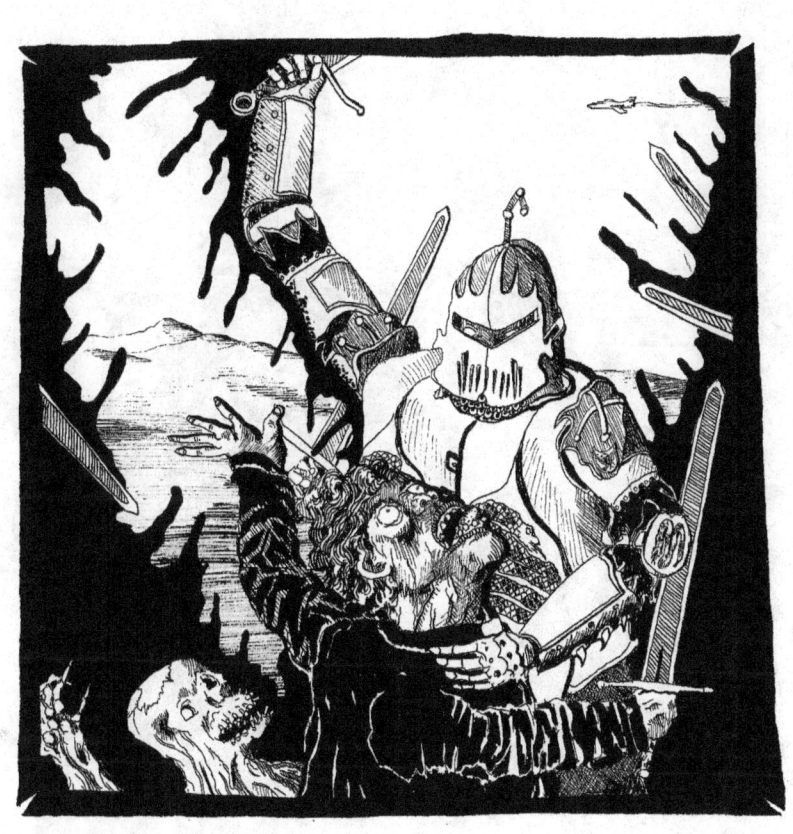

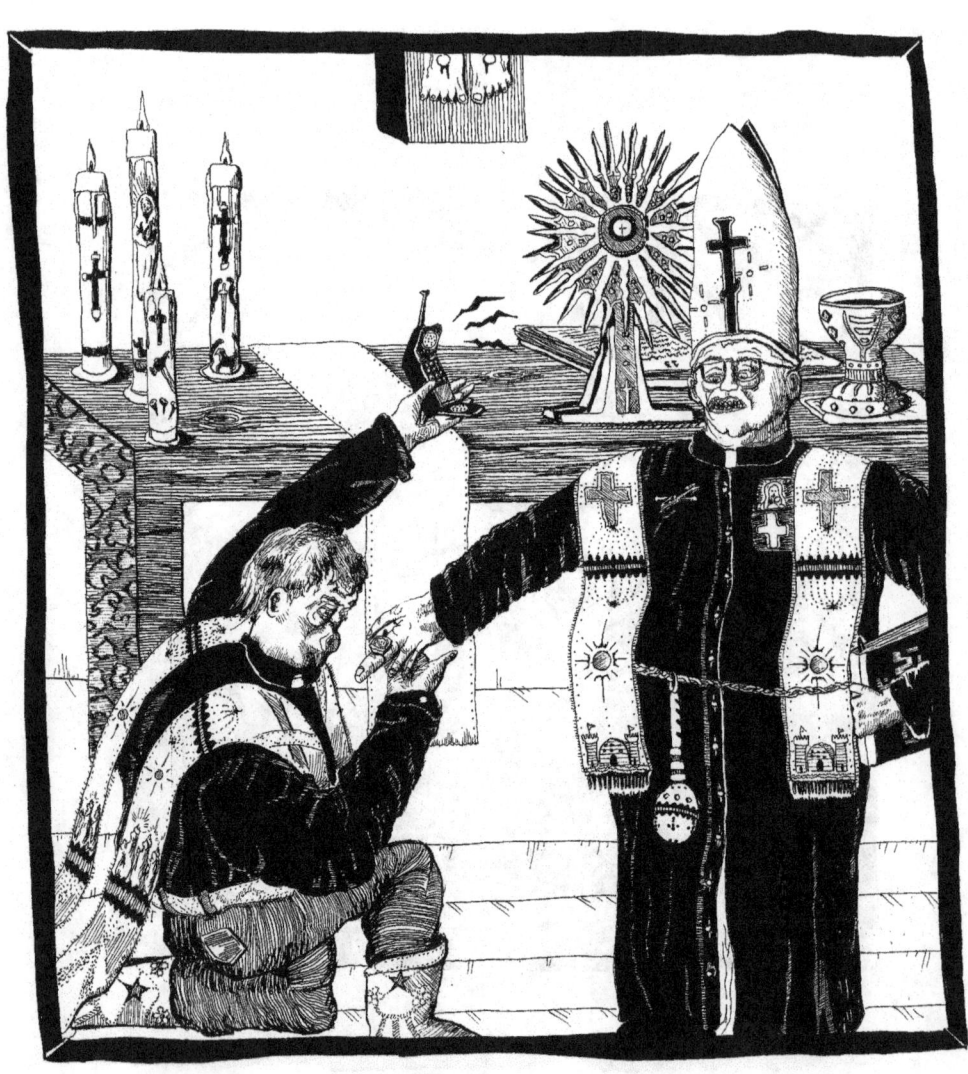

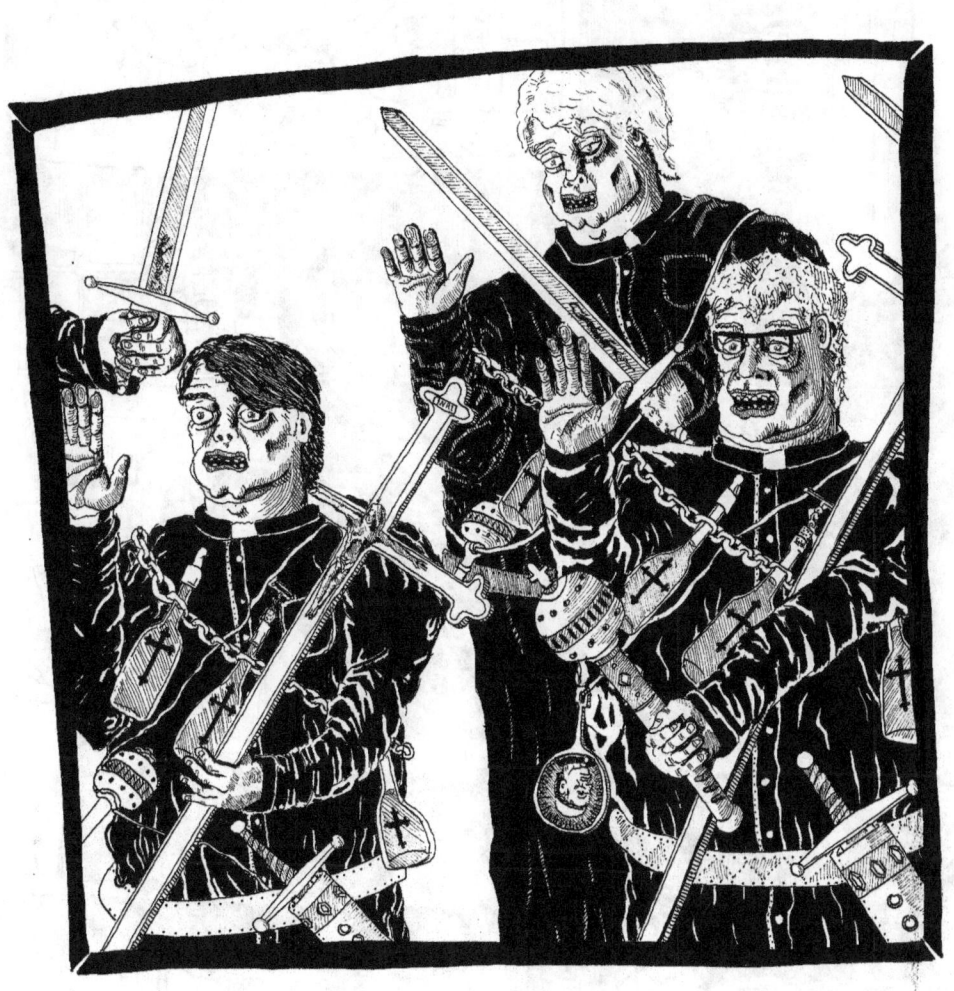

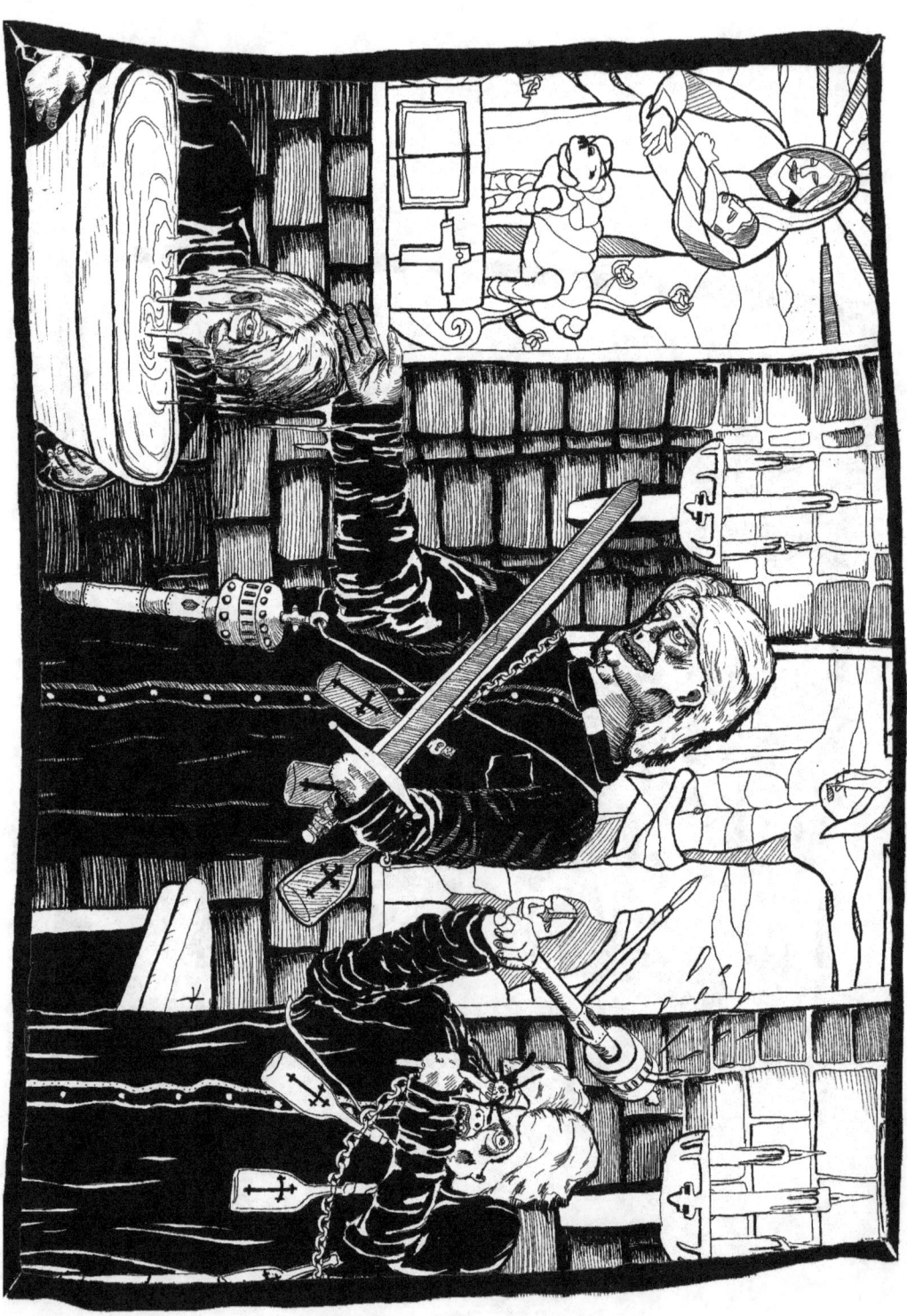

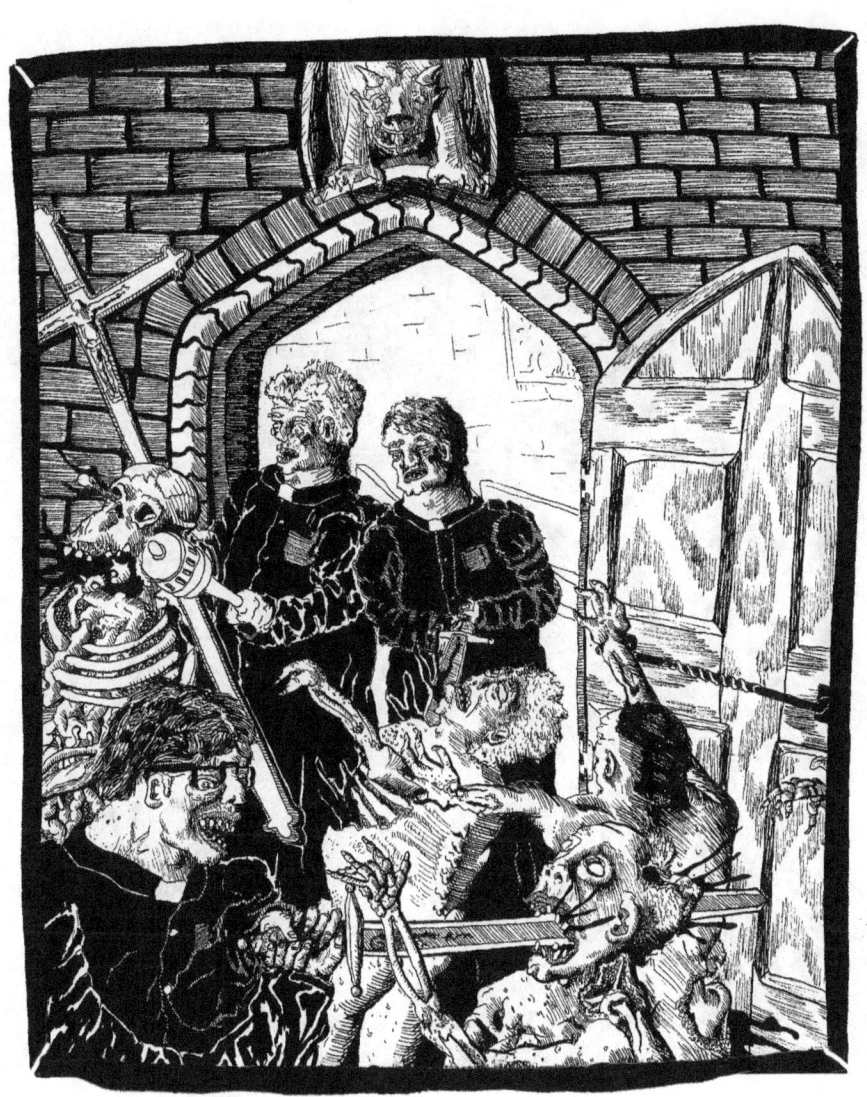

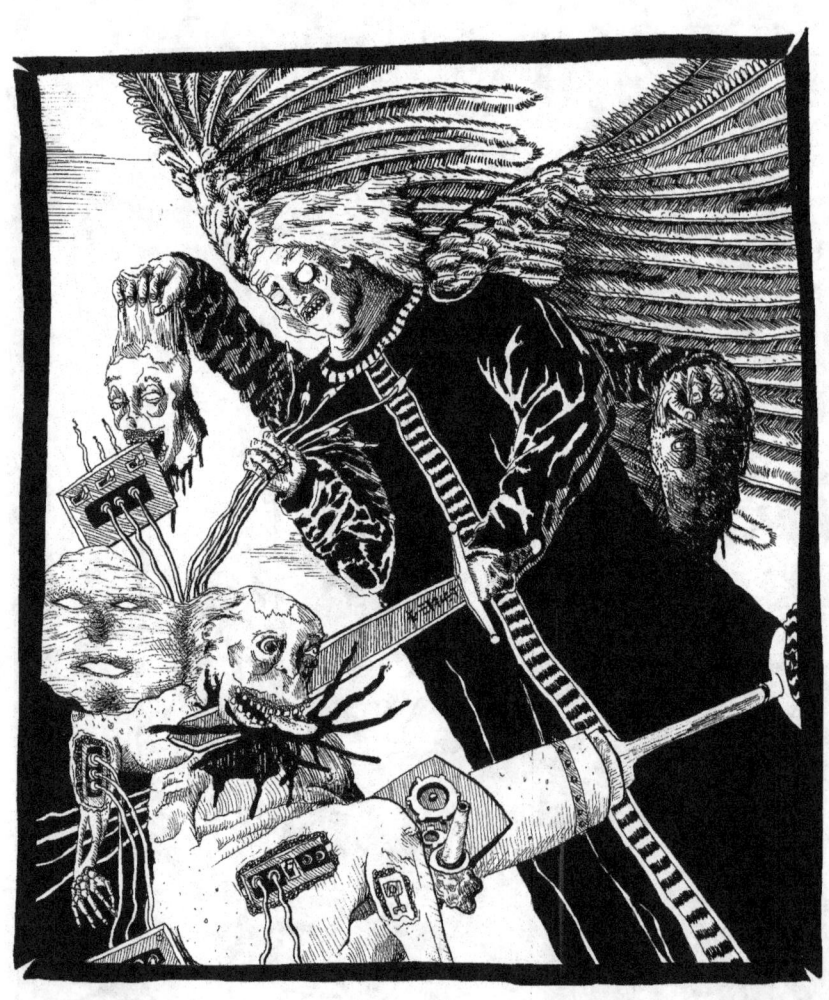

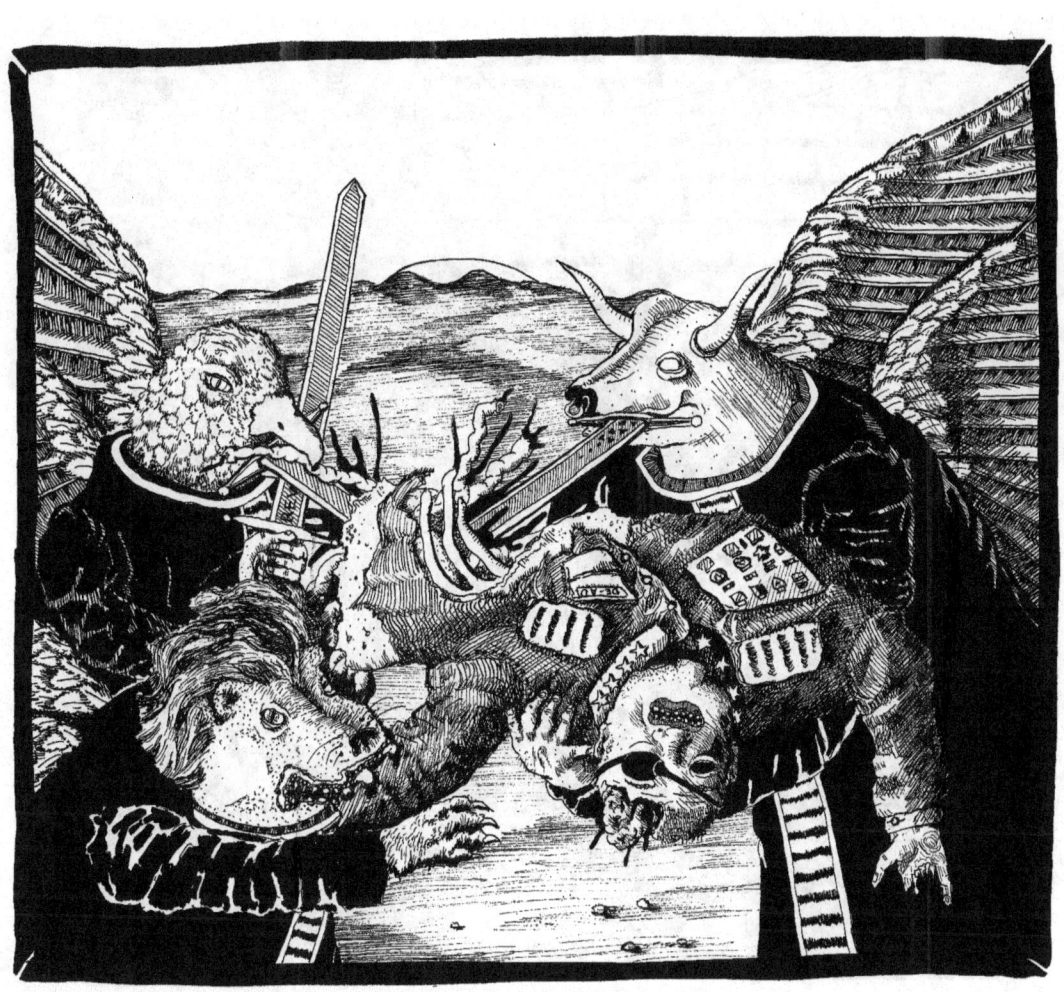

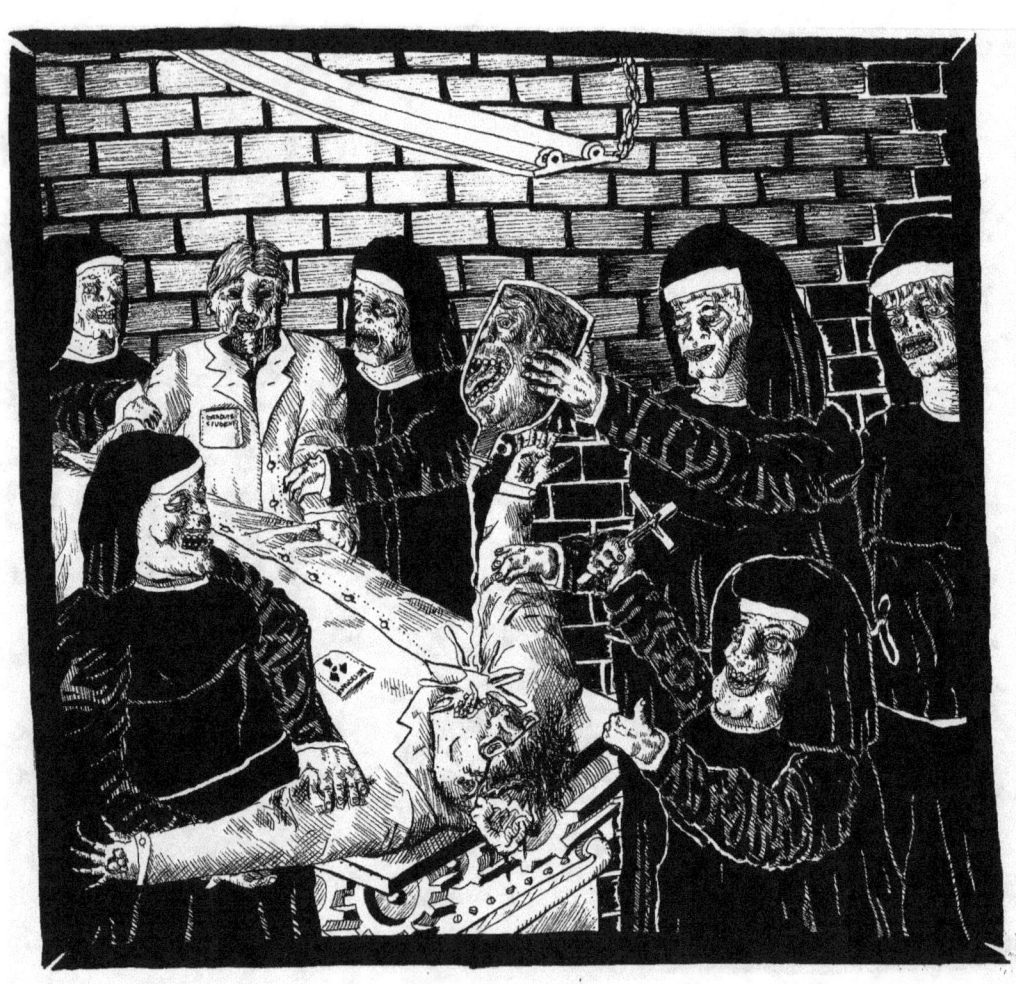

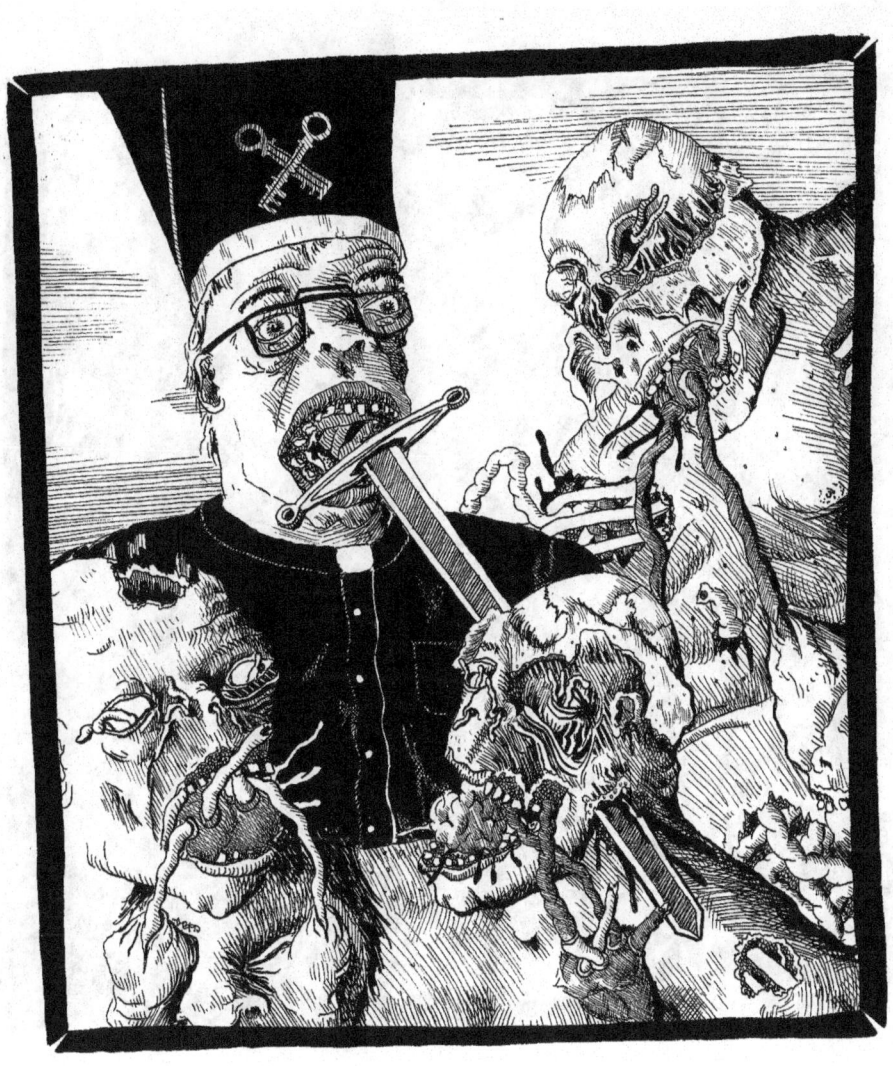

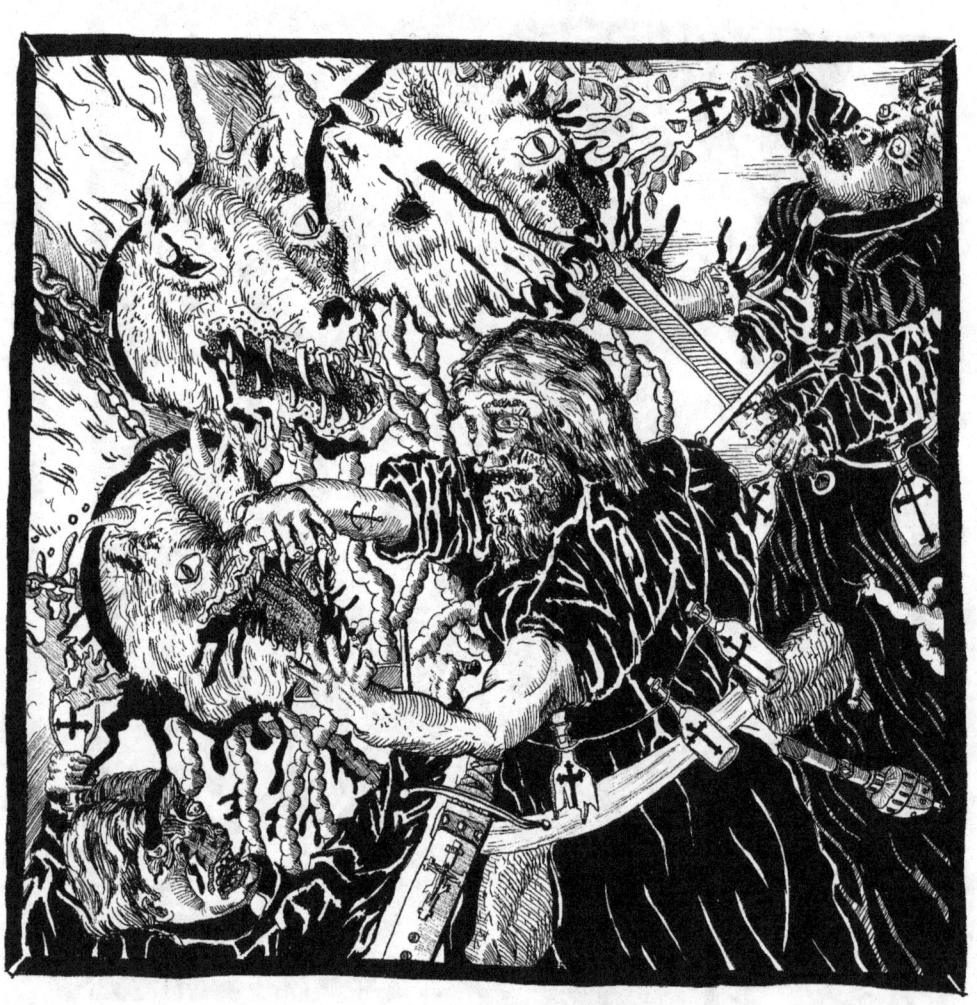

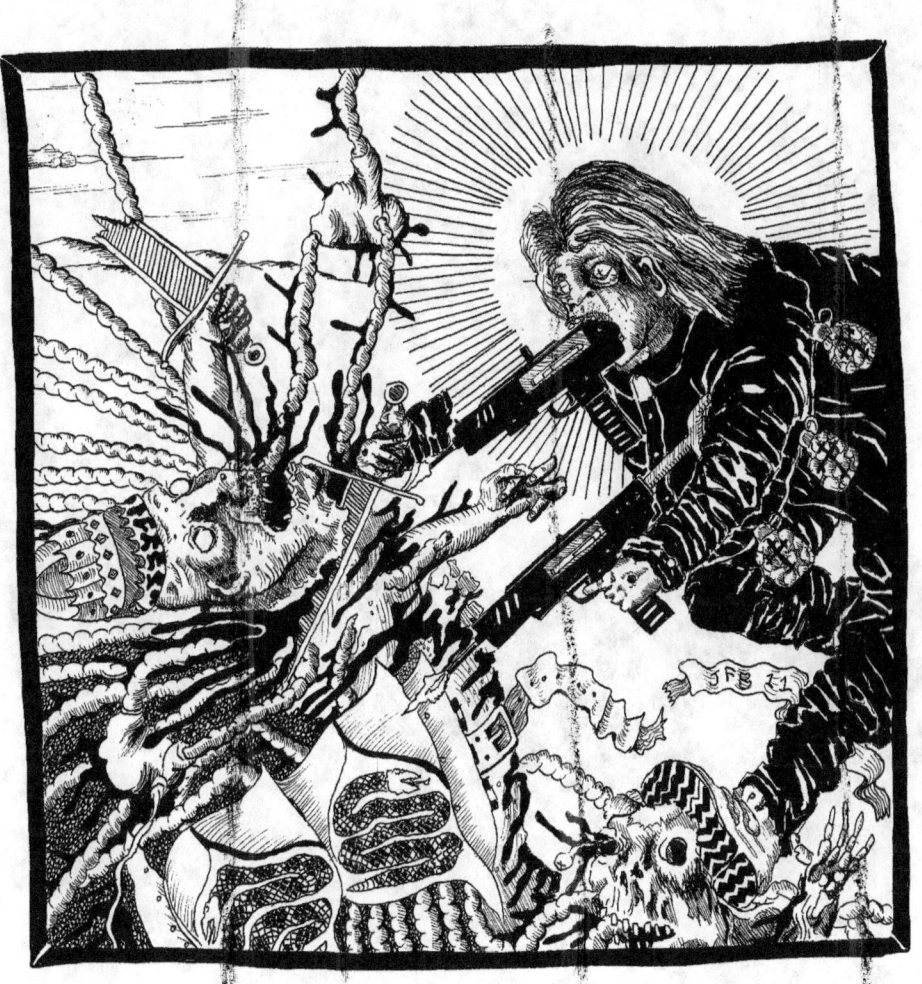

NOTES ON ZOMBIES

My opinions on Demonic Possession and the Hopeless...

Zombies are classified into two categories: the natural and the supernatural. The former manifestation seems to be portrayed most often as some kind of an infectious virus. Current zombie creators emphatically embrace the natural zombie because of a cultural rise in atheism... They wrongly assume that if the zombie seems more realistic then it is scarier. The problem with the natural zombie is that the fear produced by it is more akin to the fear of Alzheimer's rather than the fear of the "living dead." Natural zombies don't die and rise again. A natural zombie cannot have an unquenchable desire for brains. The natural zombie is simply a fully alive human being with an altered mental state that has an entirely quenchable need for ATP. This zombie is castrated and boring... literally as before, an old man dying from Alzheimer's or Dementia who seems to be particularly mean spirited when it comes to his daily intake of flesh colored mush...If this zombie eats your sister, rest assured, it will be full and take a nap. All you need to kill the asshole is a sharp sword and some common sense. To prove my point, most new zombie films don't even focus on the fear of the zombie, but rather on the fear of societal collapse... One is at more risk from fellow humans when natural zombies invade.

If the masses would embrace anything other than atheism they would be able to see that the supernatural zombie is far superior. Supernatural zombies are unpredictable; they fly, have truly unquenchable lusts for blood, flesh, and brains... If you chop off the supernatural zombies arm you create an arm that can think on its own and attack rather than just an arm that spontaneously contracts...

My book focuses on the supernatural zombie and I would argue there is only one form of supernatural zombie, the demonic zombie. Atheism robs the zombie of its spirit and I want to give it back. Possessed meat is the only true manifestation of the "living dead" because here a body can die, allowing a new spirit to enter, with which they can live again and kill. I find this zombie much more terrifying. The supernatural zombie is actually dead and therefore can never be killed... They can only be fought with exorcism... and even if you exorcise one, you still have to worry about "Legion."

A supernatural zombie should be far more terrifying to the atheist because the faithless have no tool to survive. Atheists are hopeless.

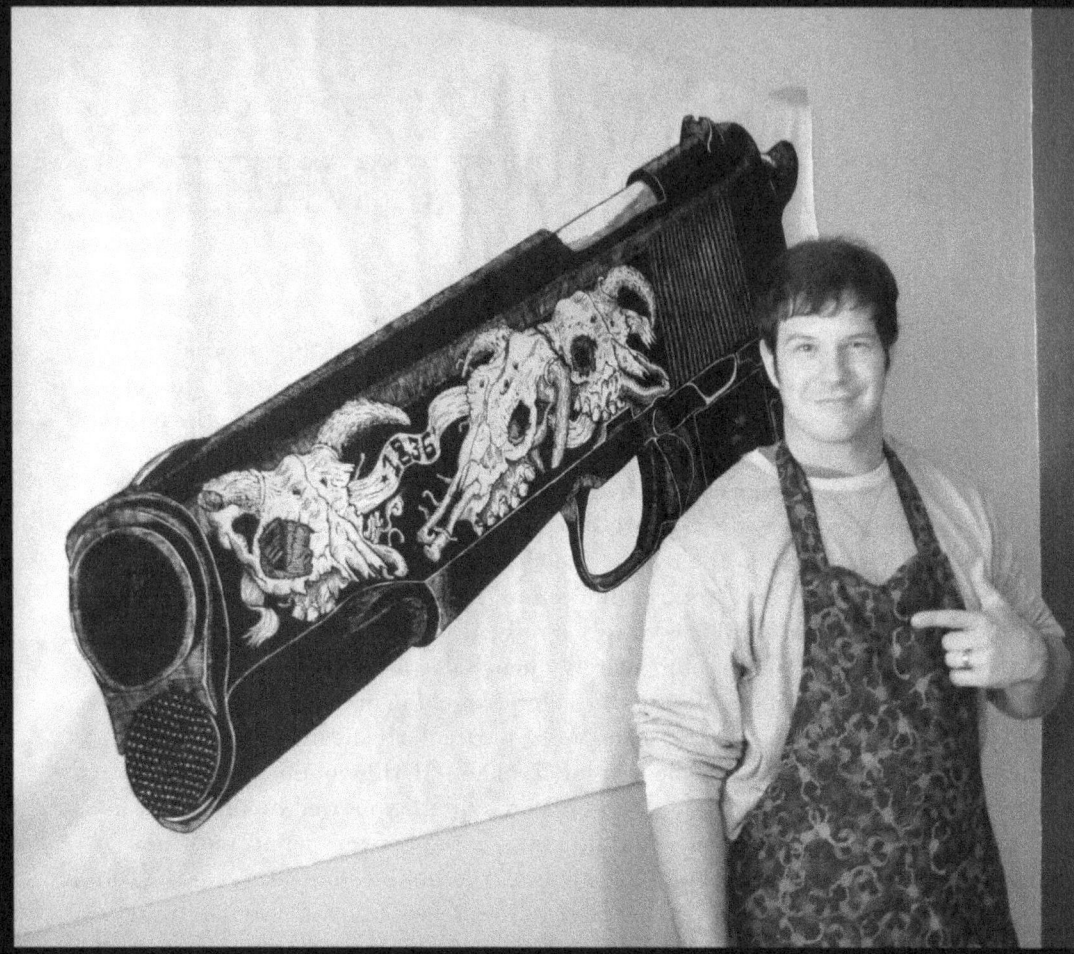

John Beckmann is a Twin Cities based printmaking artist. He grew up and went to high school in Faribault, Minnesota where he played football and swam. Later, he attended college and graduated *Summa Cum Laude* from the University of Minnesota in 2009 with dual bachelor's degrees in Physiology and Art. Currently John is studying to receive his doctorate in Entomology. His research focuses on mosquito sperm and the reproductive parasite, *Wolbachia*.

John lives in St. Paul with his wife, daughter, and Newfoundland.

Other titles from:

stampedepress.com

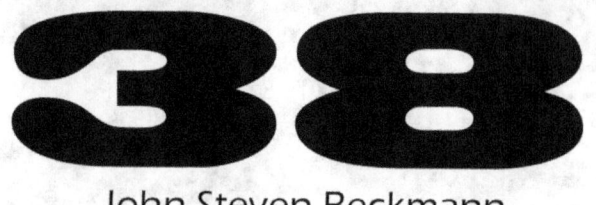

38

John Steven Beckmann

Here were hanged 38 Sioux Indians Dec. 26, 1862

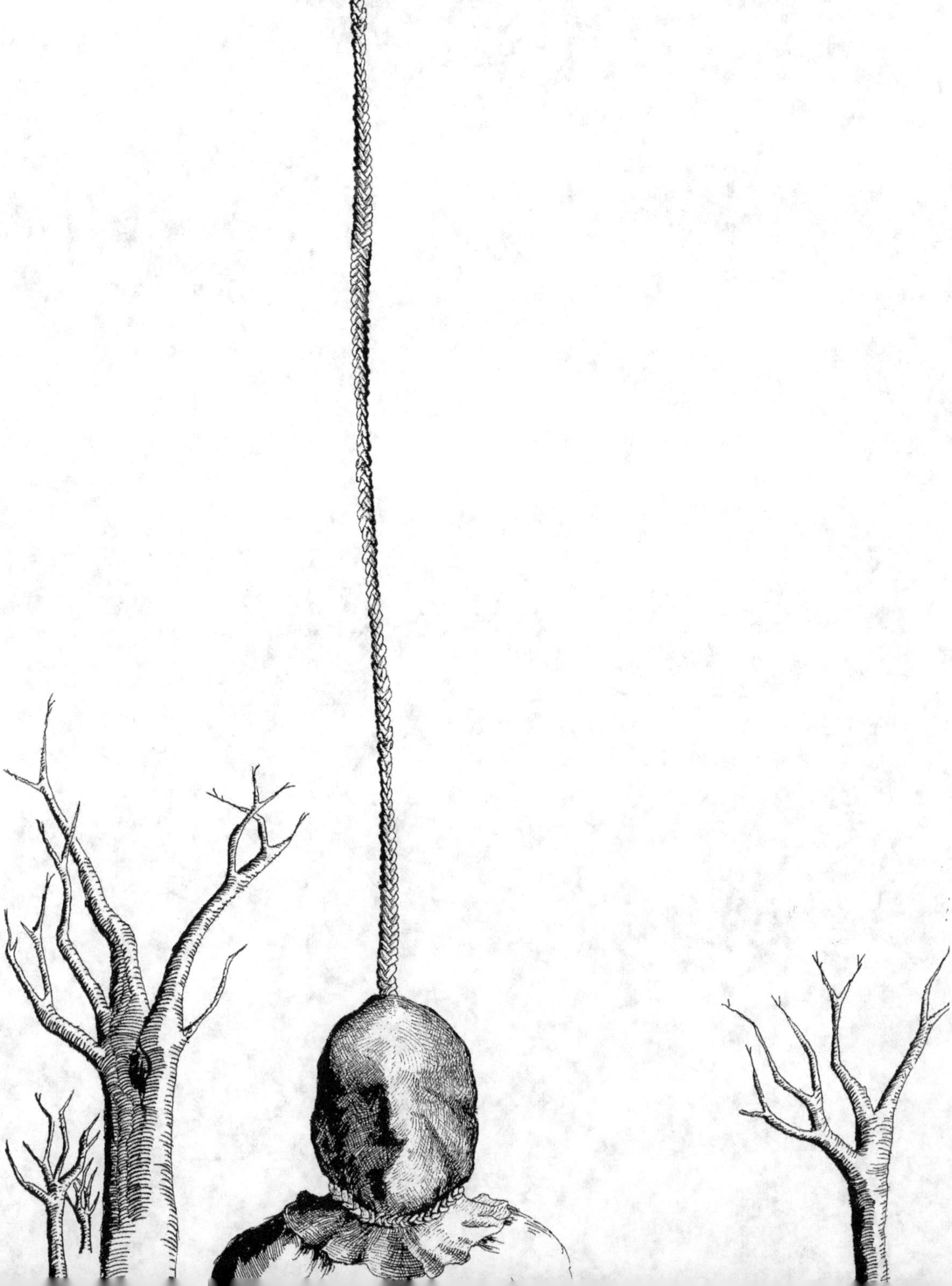